Journeying towards Jesus
in Advent

Denis McBride

redemptorist
publications

By the same author

Praying with Pictures
Borrowing the Eyes of Others: Reflecting with Paintings, Volume I
Awakening to Yourself: Reflecting with Paintings, Volume II
Journeying with Jesus: a Companion's Guide
Journeying with Jesus: a Companion's Guide for Groups
Where Does the Jesus Story Begin?
Waiting on God
Jesus and the Gospels
Seasons of the Word: Reflections on the Sunday Readings
The Parables of Jesus
Impressions of Jesus
The Gospel of Mark
The Gospel of Luke
Emmaus: the Gracious Visit of God

Reflecting with Paintings – set of 15 reflections on CD
Where Does the Jesus Story Begin? – set of 10 lectures on CD
Jesus and the Gospels – set of 36 lectures on CD

Visit: www.denismcbride.com

For my two confrères
who share community life,
Fr George Webster and Bro. Anthony McKell,
who kindly and patiently endure
my midnight hours of scribbling

Copyright © Redemptorist Publications, 2010

Published by **Redemptorist Publications**
Alphonsus House, Chawton, Hampshire, GU34 3HQ UK
Tel. +44 (0)1420 88222, Fax. +44 (0)1420 88805
email rp@rpbooks.co.uk, www.rpbooks.co.uk
A Registered Charity limited by guarantee.
Registered in England 3261721.

First published September 2010

Layout and cover design by Rosemarie Pink
Front cover illustration from istockphoto

ISBN 978-0-85231-382-4

A CIP catalogue record for this book is available from the British Library

Printed by Lithgo Press Limited, Leicester LE8 6NU

The Advent Journey

Approaching Advent

Dear Reader,

One of the advantages of writing a book is that you reach people you would never otherwise meet. As a writer you never know where your book will land, though you know it will eventually disappear in a cloud of unknowing. Whoever you are and wherever you are, dear reader, a warm welcome to these reflections on the season of Advent.

As we approach Advent we face a new liturgical year, leaving another year behind us. This season resets the clocks and calendars of Christian worship as Advent summons us to a new beginning. And as we move towards Christmas time people worry about all sorts of things. I don't know about you, but these are some of the questions I've heard and some I ask myself:

- Will the weather hold up?
- Where will we go at Christmas?
- Should we attend church?
- Will we survive the relatives and in-laws coming to stay?
- Will we eat or drink too much, say the wrong thing?

- Will we manage a smile when we open the gift wrapping?
- Will we still manage after unwrapping the third pair of seasonal socks?
- Will we survive Christmas dinner without someone saying, "I never liked you anyway!"?
- Will it be a dreary old time or a good time?
- What will we remember of this Christmas?
- Will this Christmas have anything remotely to do with Christ?

And, of course, there is the worry about presents, about what to give this one or that one; and you hear relatives and friends politely checking your pyjama size or your slipper size for predictable gifts. One mother told me she knew she was getting old when one of her children solemnly presented her with a set of thermal underwear for Christmas. (She binned it, she told me, in protest.)

The high streets start in late October with all the decorative paraphernalia, ensuring

that by the time the real feast of Christmas arrives, everyone is weary of Christmas trees and fairy lights and decorations and canned carols. The retail theatre is putting on another show; it's now time to move on to a different drama, to the Boxing Day sales and promises of bargains galore. To say nothing of the opportunity to return those woefully misjudged presents.

While the commercial world is delighted to borrow this Christian feast for its own purposes, it is shy about admitting the reason behind the festivities. Images of the birth of Christ rarely appear in shop windows: scenes from fairy tales or smiling vampires in moonlight or Santa's secret castle are much more likely to be

displayed for people's wonder. Cards tend to proclaim "Season's Greetings" rather than "Happy Christmas" – lest anyone imagine for a moment that a Christian festival is being celebrated, lest anyone get agitated about the trading world promoting a politically incorrect religious memory. And, of course, it follows, inevitably, that Easter is really about bunny rabbits and decorated eggs.

If observant Martians came to interpret our Christmas and Easter festivities, they would be hard pressed, unless they were archaeologists or palaeontologists, to uncover the original meaning of the festivals.

The Church's liturgy of Advent has a hard time competing with larger and louder signs and symbols. The liturgy's visual concession to have an Advent wreath and the gradual lighting of four or five candles seems somewhat tame compared to the explosion of ornamental lights switched on by celebrities, followed by exorbitant displays of decorations. Why wait four weeks, through the end of November and most of December, to see four candles lit when you can see an instant eruption of light fantastic in late October?

The commercial world has stolen the signs and symbols of Advent and converted them into supporting a lucrative business.

The Advent liturgy has become "a still small voice" in the midst of the clamorous proclamation of the high street. The real cathedrals seem to be the shopping centres where people flock; people's real devotions seem to be centred on hunting not for something they really need but for something to want, to fill some nameless vacancy; the liturgical readings and images for the season, for many people, are supplied by glossy magazines like *Hello!*

Gathering weekly in church to celebrate the cycle of the Advent liturgy has the feel of a diminishing protest about it. Observing the Advent season has become an act of stubborn faith to honour the birth of Jesus in the midst of collective forgetfulness. When it comes to Advent and Christmas we live in a culture of elected amnesia.

At the heart of the Advent season is the recognition that we are a people unashamedly centred on God, waiting for God; we gather to celebrate the coming of God in Jesus and wait for the return of Jesus at the end of time. As we look back and look forward in the liturgy there is structured dissent from the pervading culture that everything that is of value is happening now. We express our belief, through a community setting of narration and performance, that we all have a greater power than ourselves to genuflect before, something grander than our own experience to bow down before, something higher than our own insight to acknowledge, something that is beyond us yet is mysteriously part of ourselves.

During Advent we confess our own incompleteness and acknowledge that there is always more to God than what we can know or believe or sense. In that recognition there is a proclamation of hope in the majestic goodness of God: in waiting we declare our hope in God's kind purposes.

The season of Advent gives us time to reflect, to look back and to look forward. This book is written in the hope that it might be a companion to the season and help you journey towards the great moment of the birth of Christ. I have followed the movement of the season. In the first week we look forward to the coming of Christ at the end of the world, a subject rarely mentioned even in church. In the second week we look at the towering figure of John the Baptist, who prepared for the coming of the Messiah. In the third week we celebrate the quiet man of Christianity, Joseph, who followed many diversions before he eventually arrived to make a home for his family in Nazareth. In the fourth week we celebrate Mary, the young girl who welcomed the unexpected in God's plan for her and for humanity. In the final chapter we celebrate Christmas as the feast that challenges us to move from being onlookers at the manger to being active followers of Jesus.

I have selected a number of paintings and pictures to enliven the text, in the hope that they might add their own meaning to the words. Finally I would like to thank Trish Wilson, our marketing manager at Redemptorist Publications, for her suggestion to write these reflections; and Rosemarie Pink, our supervisor in the design studio, for her distinctive talent and her patience in designing this book. Without her skill, this book would look very dull indeed.

Sincerely,

Denis McBride C.Ss.R.
Alphonsus House
Chawton
Hampshire
GU34 3HQ

Preparing for the end

First week in Advent

Preparing for the end
Jesus, the kind counsellor

"It all happened so quickly"

The liturgical readings for the first week in Advent focus on the end of the world, a subject that engages few people in our world except perhaps those who are apprehensive about a nuclear holocaust. Pious maxims such as "Live every day as if it's your last" have little purchasing power on the modern mind. We tend to be a generation fixated on the present moment: the here and now, not eternity, is what engages our interest. As one single mother of three children said to me recently: "It takes me all my time to get through the day. Eternity will be getting through tomorrow."

Yet we know from experience that some people's lives are cancelled without warning, without thought, without ceremony. An abrupt ending, neither imagined nor anticipated, interrupts life terminally – fatal natural disasters, fatal accidents, fatal conflicts. Nearly always the word "fatal" is a description that arrives after the event. While this doesn't signal the end of the world, it effectively extinguishes individual worlds. In the words of Jesus:

"I tell you, on that night there will be two in one bed; one will be taken and the other left. There will be two women grinding meal together; one will be taken and the other left."
(Luke 17:34-35)

When catastrophe happens, the ones who are left behind attend the aftermath as dumb witnesses, their eyes fixed on some undefined horizon, lost in their own secret world of loss. After a while they return home, warily and uneasily, to the remains of their own lives and the freakish fact that they have survived. Survivor's guilt (or "survivor's syndrome") is a complex psychological condition that mostly revolves around the fact that the survivor lived on, a realisation that often induces not profound relief but self-loathing and even self-destruction. For many, it is tied to the random fact that while others died, maybe traumatically, they themselves did not. This can bring on severe depression, anxiety and despair, each masked or expressed in a variety of ways.

Some years ago, when I was lecturing at St Louis University in Baguio City,

Journey — Preparing — Investing — Adjusting — Welcoming — Celebrating

in the Philippines, a friend of mine, Fr Lode Wostyn, drove me up to a beautiful sightseeing spot, deep in the Baguio mountains. We were admiring the view, absorbing the uncut silence, when a car with darkened windows slowly pulled off the road and parked near us. The car sat there, souped-up engine reverberating, shaded windows revealing nothing.

Lode told me to get into our car, but, as soon as we made a move, four masked men jumped out of the darkened car, armed with guns: two of them stationed themselves in the middle of the road to block any traffic approaching from either direction; the other two advanced towards us, commanding us to put our arms in the air. We obligingly did.

One of them went around the car, shooting out the four tyres – I had never heard gunfire at such close quarters – and then climbed into the car to collect anything he could find of value. The other gunman waved his pistol between Lode and me, warning us in Tagalog not to make a move – a superfluous instruction, since neither of us could command a muscle. With the return of the tyre liquidator, we now had the devoted attention of a single gunman each, who relieved us of our bags and wallets, then searched around our trouser belts in case we had secreted money bags.

When the gunman attending me had assured himself that I had nothing more to give, including inspecting my empty shoes, he walked a few paces, turned round to face me, and raised his pistol, aiming it at my head. I looked into the barrel. This was it, I thought, a summary execution in the middle of nowhere. And yes, my life did pass before me in a few seconds, although I have to admit that the brief film was deeply disappointing. Suddenly a voice commanded from the road, and the four gunmen turned, ran, jumped into the car and sped off, tyres squealing, leaving Lode and myself speechlessly relieved we were still alive, but without wheels to tell the tale.

It all happened so quickly – probably within fifty seconds.

The little traffic that had been stopped, including two jeepneys, the popular local

transport, now eased forward to inspect the scene of the crime. In no hurry to go anywhere, a real drama within reach, people piled out to express their ready sympathy, kindly enquiring about how we were feeling. Neither Lode nor I felt like giving a rundown on our emotional temperature, and we looked across, vacantly, at each other. One man, I remember, after circling our car to inspect the damage, joked that zapping all four tyres was on the excessive side. I think I might have smiled. We were offered a lift, which we agreed to take to the nearest police station in La Trinidad. There we related our story of the robbery carried out with military-style precision:

Journey Preparing Investing Adjusting Welcoming Celebrating

we offered vague descriptions of the hooded men and the car; useless notes were taken down; promises were made; then we were driven home to Baguio.

A deep sense of relief that we had survived the robbery with our lives was the governing feeling we both shared. Later that day, however, when I heard that the same four gunmen had, previous to our hold-up, robbed and fatally shot a Chinese money changer, the sense of relief moved to something else: the question, "Why did we survive and he did not?" With this news, everything changed. The fact that he had resisted and paid a terminal price was not the issue: we had been held up by the same men but survived to tell the tale. Why so?

The awkward transition from relief to guilt is something that I can notionally accept makes sense, although the guilt has never gone away. Psychological insight does not necessarily solve anything nor soothe troubled souls. In the rare recurrence of the event in dreams, I still wait for that pointed gun to go off. Close friends tell me it will get easier. It doesn't; it just gets later.

Of course, those of us who happen to be living are all survivors – for now. But the day or the night will surely come when we cease to survive and are embraced by death. How and when that will happen none of us is given to know; we know only that it will, inevitably, take place. When it does, will we have a sense of a completed life? Will we be able to look back at our lives and say, "By and large, all things considered, it was a good life"? How will we judge our lives? What criteria will we use to assess our life as worthwhile or discount it as a wasted opportunity? How will we brave our own last judgement?

Preparing

Gospel text: Matthew 25:31-46

When the Son of Man comes in his glory, and all the angels with him, then he will sit on the throne of his glory. All the nations will be gathered before him, and he will separate people one from another as a shepherd separates the sheep from the goats, and he will put the sheep at his right hand and the goats at the left.

Then the king will say to those at his right hand, "Come, you that are blessed by my Father, inherit the kingdom prepared for you from the foundation of the world; for I was hungry and you gave me food, I was thirsty and you gave me something to drink, I was a stranger and you welcomed me, I was naked and you gave me clothing, I was sick and you took care of me, I was in prison and you visited me."

Then the righteous will answer him, "Lord, when was it that we saw you hungry and gave you food, or thirsty and gave you something to drink? And when was it that we saw you a stranger and welcomed you, or naked and gave you clothing? And when was it that we saw you sick or in prison and visited you?" And the king will answer them, "Truly I tell you, just as you did it to one of the least of these who are members of my family, you did it to me."

Then he will say to those at his left hand, "You that are accursed, depart from me into the eternal fire prepared for the devil and his angels; for I was hungry and you gave me no food, I was thirsty and you gave me nothing to drink, I was a stranger and you did not welcome me, naked and you did not give me clothing, sick and in prison and you did not visit me."

Then they also will answer, "Lord, when was it that we saw you hungry or thirsty or a stranger or naked or sick or in prison, and did not take care of you?" Then he will answer them, "Truly I tell you, just as you did not do it to one of the least of these, you did not do it to me." And these will go away into eternal punishment, but the righteous into eternal life.

Journey — Preparing — Investing — Adjusting — Welcoming — Celebrating

Reflecting on the Gospel story

Beginning at the end

Faced by the disciples' worry about the last times, Jesus kindly gives them an insight into the last challenge we will all face. The discourse is given only to the disciples and has its climax in the apocalyptic vision of the last judgement. Apocalypse may seem a strange place for us to begin, but endings can make for new beginnings: *the future is revealed to help us to live genuine lives today.* The Greek word *apokalypsis* literally means "uncovering"; it is the act of removing the covering that conceals something, thereby exposing it to view. The apocalyptic vision of the last judgement unveils a truth that is hidden – not to satisfy any fitful curiosity about the future tense but to challenge us, hearers and readers, about the values we live by in the present tense.

The last judgement provokes the question: if that is how we will be judged at the end of time, how should we live our lives today?

The last judgement refuses to see the future as a fateful accident or humanity as its hapless victim; rather, it uncovers the truth that our future will be the direct consequence of the everyday choices we make. In that sense the teaching attempts to make us conscious choice-makers in favour of those who are disadvantaged. Who we become in the fullness of time will depend on the choices we make and the values we choose to govern our lives.

The gathering

The gathering is the assembly of humanity, presided over by the supreme king of all peoples, who has taken his seat on his glorious throne. He has dominion over all and has, therefore, the right to judge all, a right that has been conferred on him by God: "All authority in heaven and on earth has been given to me" (Matthew 28:18). Among those who are assembled there is no distinction or discrimination between races or religions, between Jew and Gentile, between priest and lay, between man and woman. There is no hierarchy, no privilege and no precedence. What the assembled people share is their common bond of humanity, so that when the king/shepherd makes the separation, he will be separating the people as individuals, not as national or religious groupings.

The separation and the judgement

Although this is a judgement scene, there is no trial procedure. The trial has taken place during the life of each person and

the judgement has already been made; the only outstanding business is to pass sentence. In the detail from Burne-Jones' stained glass window of the last judgement, we see a group of people, dressed in many colours, anxiously awaiting the sentence of judgement. The sense of anticipation is enhanced by their gestures. We see two fearful women clasp each other while a man hides behind one woman's blue cloak.

The imagery of the parable shifts momentarily from king to shepherd to match the parabolic imagery of the assembly as a gathered flock. The image of a shepherd separating sheep from goats was a regular, rather than a final, occurrence in Palestinian life. As Joachim Jeremias notes: "The Palestinian shepherd does not separate sheep from rams (i.e. the females from the males), but sheep from the goats, since the goats need to be kept warm at night, for cold harms them, while the sheep prefer open air at night."[1] In the scenario of the parable, however, the separation is final as it constitutes eternal judgement.

The sheep are placed on the right, the goats on the left. The customary use of

[1] J. Jeremias, *The Parables of Jesus* (London: SCM, 1972), 206.

"right and left understanding" in popular lore is brought into play, where right is distinguished from left as honesty from treachery, blessing from curse, and good fortune from bad luck. Unfortunately for left-handed people, this dualism has been carried into the English language: thus when people's actions are described as

dextrous (from the Latin *dexter*, "on the right hand") it means that what is done is adroit, skilful, subtle; whereas if what is done is described as sinister (from the Latin *sinister*, "on the left hand"), it is underhand, malign, suggesting the threat of evil.

The king welcomes those on his right hand with the words: "Come, you that are blessed by my Father, inherit the kingdom prepared for you from the foundation of the world." Just as the land of Israel was granted by God to God's chosen people, so now the new people of God are granted the kingdom as their inheritance. Those who are reckoned blessed take possession of the only kingdom that has outlasted the world. Throughout the turmoil of history and in spite of the defiance of humankind, God's abiding purpose was never frustrated: God's kingdom stands secure and ready for those who have distinguished themselves by acts of mercy.

In the judgement the only division made is between those who connected themselves to people in need and those who remained disconnected from them. People are welcomed as "blessed by my Father" because they have paid attention not to the Father or the Son but to the legion of

vulnerable people within their reach. Six categories of people in distress are listed, together with six appropriate responses.

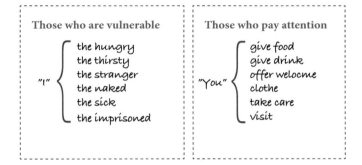

Those who are vulnerable		Those who pay attention	
"I"	the hungry the thirsty the stranger the naked the sick the imprisoned	"You"	give food give drink offer welocme clothe take care visit

In the left-hand column there is a list of vulnerable human beings whose needs await recognition and practical help, together with the startling revelation that Jesus' presence abides among them. In the right-hand column there is a list of humane responses by the just, together with the startling revelation that Jesus himself was the beneficiary of these acts of kindness. Those who are blessed are commended for their actions, not their attitudes; for what they did, not for what they thought. Misery obliged them to act, so their active verbs prove to be what is important. Their response was humane and, therefore, profoundly religious; it is hallowed as

the kingdom response of those who take responsibility for a broken world.

In his reflections on humanity, the distinguished Jewish philosopher Abraham Heschel makes a distinction between human being and being human: while we are all human beings, being human is something we become or fail to become. Humanity is not a given but a goal for every human being. He writes:

> "The degree to which one is sensitive to other people's suffering, to other men's humanity, is the index of one's own humanity. It is the root not only for social living but for the study of humanities... The central problem of biblical thinking is not: 'What is to be?' but rather: 'How to be and how not to be?'"[2]

That, it seems to me, is the question of the last judgement. Those that are blessed are commended for their humane solidarity with those who suffer loss. No special training or charismatic gift or even religious insight was needed to equip them for their ministry of mercy. They are acclaimed, for example, for doing the ordinary round of visiting those

[2] A.J. Heschel, *Who is Man?* (Stanford, CA: Stanford University Press, 1975), 46-47.

who are sick and imprisoned, not for the extraordinary ministry of healing those who are afflicted and liberating prisoners. The expectation is that these works of mercy are within the capacity of every human being: that all people, no matter what their racial or religious background, can administer this practical care. Those that are blessed did precisely that.

That is why, in this universal judgement, there is no mention of great heroics; there are no stories of conquest, no tales of remarkable virtue, no outstanding triumphs over disaster; in fact there is no specifically religious note sounded. The actions are the simple response of those who pay attention to what happens in the world of the familiar and who move to answer the needs that confront them. For Jesus, what happens in the world of the familiar has an eternity of importance about it. Human graciousness and kindness are grounds enough for welcome into the fullness of the kingdom. In this understanding, religion is not about a privatised relationship with God, independent of those who suffer around us. People's suffering is not considered a distraction from God's purposes; rather, their suffering incarnates the agenda for a kingdom people.

Those on the king's left hand are called accursed and then condemned to "the eternal fire prepared for the devil and his angels". Although the imagery of fire for future punishment has no history in ancient Hebrew thought, Matthew has already spoken of the Gehenna of fire (Matthew 5:22; 18:9). The word Gehenna originally referred to the valley of Hinnom, a narrow gorge that curves along the west and south of Jerusalem. The valley was the scene of the idolatrous worship of the gods Molech and Baal, who, it was believed, could only be placated by children being burned in sacrifice on "the high place of Topheth" (Jeremiah 7:31; see 19:4-6). The valley's association with fire arose not only from the sacrificial cult of Molech but from the fires that continually burned there when the valley became a rubbish dump. Isaiah prophesied that the site would be readied for Molech himself (Isaiah 30:33), and he spoke about an unquenchable fire prepared for the wicked (Isaiah 33:14; 66:24). By the first century AD, however, Gehenna had become divorced from its geographical location as a rubbish dump to become hell itself.

As those that are blessed are not praised for heroic virtues, those that are cursed are

not accused of great offences or violent crimes: they are condemned because of their failure to be humane to those in need. The principle of judgement is the same for everyone, and the list of those who are needy remains unchanged.

The protest: "When did we see you… ?"
Those who are blessed are not conscious of having done any special service to the king (Jesus). Their surprise is expressed by the question "But when did we see you…?" Commenting on Egyptian and rabbinic parallels, Jeremias observes:

> "Both in the Egyptian Book of the Dead and in the Midrash the dead man boasts self-confidently of his good deeds ('I have given satisfaction to God by doing that in which he delights: I have given bread to the hungry, water to the thirsty, clothed the naked…'). How differently sounds the surprised question of the righteous, who are unconscious of having rendered any service, to say nothing of the conception that in the persons of the poor and wretched, men are confronted by the hidden Messiah."[3]

Those that are blessed are astounded at the revelation that the king identifies himself with those who are needy, and they protest that they never saw *him* when they performed their works of mercy. They were never conscious of ministering to Jesus, only to people in need. The king explains in his answer: "Truly, I tell you, just as you did it to one of the least of these who are members of my family, you did it to me." Who are the members of the king's family? Are they the same people as those who are needy? Or are they disciples/missionaries who form a persecuted minority within society at large?

The surprise and the ignorance of the whole gathering are more consistent with a judgement of all peoples who are being held accountable for their relationship with the needy people of the world. The assembly's surprise, it may be said, may also be reflected in the reader's astonishment that Jesus has chosen to identify himself so closely with the needy people among humanity. We as Christians are not beyond astonishment in regard to that particular revelation!

Earlier on in Matthew's Gospel Jesus allied himself with the little child over against the disciples in their concern for primacy (Matthew 18:1-6); he asked his followers not to despise the little ones (Matthew 18:10); he challenged them to change their

way of thinking about pastoral leadership and become servants: "whoever wishes to be great among you must be your servant" (Matthew 20:26). As John P. Meier comments:

> "Here [in the last judgement scene] it becomes clear that 'servant' cannot evaporate into another hierarchical title; service means the concrete performance of the loving acts listed (cf. 16:27). Because the second group has neglected such acts, it neglected the Son of Man; and so its neglect has become fatal... Christ's teaching on the twofold love of God and neighbour (22:34-40) thus undergoes a profound transformation: love of the (poor) neighbour is practically identified with love of God and receives a christological basis."[4]

That christological basis, it seems to me, is the heart of the parable's subversive teaching: kindness to those who are needy proves to be real attentiveness to Jesus.

Connection and disconnection

At the centre of the last judgement is the revelation that one way Jesus elects to be present to humanity is through the cry of those who are needy. His "I" is hidden in what might be regarded as a most unlikely

sanctuary. Imagine for a moment three alien travellers journeying from outer space aboard their starship: they are coming with the express intention of finding an unusual king who is rumoured to be living among us. The three pilgrims land unannounced on our doorstep, carrying the gifts they have brought from afar, and tell us why they have journeyed to this place: they are looking for Jesus. We cannot help but notice their curious gifts and wonder what possible use anyone could find for them, but we say nothing. Their question brings us back to their purpose: "Where", they ask, "can we find him?"

What directions would we give? We might direct them to the church, in the hope that the priests might introduce them to word and sacrament. Or we might direct them to strange sanctuaries, such as refugee camps and hospitals and prisons, and say that Jesus himself said that he was to be found among the inhabitants there. Granted, this is a bizarre scene, but it is not the visit of the aliens that makes it so.

In the apocalyptic vision of the last judgement, given to the disciples prior to his death, Jesus focuses attention on his continuing presence among vulnerable people. It is as if Jesus deliberately turns his own followers away from an exclusive attraction to himself, away from a restricted focus on his own person, to look elsewhere to find him. In so doing, he challenges us to face the pain and loss endured by others, not to keep staring at him. He will be found where others suffer.

In the parable Jesus reveals his own profound respect for those who suffer in the midst of life. At the same time he hallows the many ordinary kindnesses of those who have never heard of him – the vast majority of humankind – and claims that the way of mercy is a way to the fullness of the kingdom. The parable answers the question Christians sometimes ask: what will happen to all those unbaptised people who have never heard of Jesus the Christ, those who have never "seen" him? The parable answers that they have all met him because he has been hiding unseen in the vulnerable people they encountered in the course of their lives. There are many roads to God: connecting with mercy to the legion of needy people is one of the most sure.

The parable's emphasis on staying connected with people is one that needs

4 J.P. Meier, *Matthew* (Dublin: Veritas, 1981), 305.

to be heard particularly in today's world. In an incisive critique of British society, published in 2009, Matthew Fforde offers his review from a Christian standpoint: he regards the lack of ties and non-belonging – desocialisation – as the dominant crisis facing our modern society. Among the negative influences, he notes the rise in individualism:

"Selfish individualism involves a massive propensity to concern with the individual self. An individual's attention is turned towards himself, towards his own concerns, interests and perceptions. This inward-lookingness is compounded by the consequences of the suffering and anxiety caused by a loss of ties. The worry and care provoked in individuals by the poverty of their own human relationships, by their lack of fulfilment and by their detachment often engenders an inward-looking form of personality which has little time or concern for others... Whole areas of their inner selves are either stunted in their growth or not developed at all. A lack of authentic interaction with other people produces a failure to develop a sensitivity towards other people."[5]

In contrast to this cultural shift, the parable invites people to look outwards, to move

Journey — Preparing — Investing — Adjusting — Welcoming — Celebrating

beyond the boundaries of their own defined worlds, to notice and connect with those in need. The parable is a protest against abandoning those in need to anonymity, a protest against a culture of retrenchment where many seem to be slowly but surely shifting away from a sense of obligation to other people to asserting their own rights. In the present climate, where so many are disenchanted with politics and feel alienated from institutions and authority, the parable calls us back to a sense of community and humane attentiveness to one another.

Every year thousands of people die alone and unmourned in Britain, like Andrew Smith. In an article for the *Sunday Times Magazine*, Ariel Leve wrote:

"When Andrew Smith died, nobody noticed. His flat, No 171, was at the end of the row on the second floor. His body was discovered when a neighbour, someone he had never talked to, smelt something off and phoned the police. Andrew Smith had been dead for two months... There were no details on record of next of kin, and nothing in his flat to identify family or friends... he had nobody...

"Andrew Smith must have wondered who would grieve for him or feel the loss. And to live your life knowing that if you didn't exist, nobody would notice, must be so lonely; it's being a ghost long before you have gone."[6]

Our world and society are haunted by legions of living ghosts. The parable of the last judgement is a counter-cultural call to engage in a common project of taking responsibility for those who feel defeated by life rather than leaving it to "them" – government agencies and social services. We are responsible for one another, and that responsibility will be the core question of our own judgement.

Letting the parable interpret us
When we allow the parable to interpret us, we recognise that sometimes we are in the right-hand column – among those who try to pay attention and stay connected to those who are vulnerable. There are times, of course, when we ignore them; but there are times when we inhabit the left-hand column, when we live among those who hunger and thirst – not for food and drink, perhaps, but for other basic essentials that give life. There are times when we all feel disconnected from others.

[5] M. Fforde, *Desocialisation: The Crisis of Post-Modernity* (Cheadle Hulme: Gabriel, 2009), 256-257.
[6] A. Leve, "Broken Pieces of a Lost Life", *Sunday Times Magazine*, 2 September 2007, 19.

We hunger and thirst	to be wanted and to be loved to be affirmed and encouraged to live in peace and know justice.
We are naked	when everyone knows our failure when we are exposed in our sin/weakness when we lose our good name.
We are the stranger	when we feel like the permanent outsider when we are excluded because of our colour/ our race/our religion/our difference when we are ignored.
We are sick	when we are burdened by anxiety or loss when the sadness is upon us when we are broken-hearted or depressed.
We are imprisoned	when we are shut inside our own loneliness when we feel hemmed in by life and misfortune when we live in permanent unemployment.

When we live inside our own suffering and loss, we hope that others will pay attention; that they will notice our plight and minister to us; that they will share their resources and resourcefulness with us. And, when they do, we always welcome their attention and kindness as good news.

When we suffer we know what good news would be for us: *our suffering defines the meaning of Gospel.*

Mother Teresa of Calcutta told a BBC interviewer why she spent her long life in caring for the people that society rejects:

"I have said this many times before but I will say it again: Jesus is present in the broken bodies of these suffering people. My way of serving him is to serve them. The biggest disease in the world today is not leprosy or AIDS, but the feeling of being unwanted and uncared for. The greatest evil is the lack of love, the terrible indifference towards one's neighbour. What the poor, and not just the poor, need even more than food, clothes and shelter, is to be wanted."

Her stubborn work on behalf of people in need during her life, and the work of those like her, might provide the most eloquent commentary on the teaching of the last judgement.

Finally, the poet Gerard Manley Hopkins celebrated the truth of the parable when he wrote:

"...for Christ plays in ten thousand places,
Lovely in limbs, and lovely in eyes not his
To the Father through the features of men's faces."[7]

[7] G.M. Hopkins, "As Kingfishers Catch Fire", in *Gerard Manley Hopkins, Poems and Prose*, ed. W.H. Gardner (Penguin: Harmondsworth, 1973), 51.

Preparing

Questions for reflection

1. In our society, who are the invisible people – the ones who are not only unattended but who go unnoticed?

2. When you review your own life, are there any groups of people that you have had particular difficulty approaching? Why did you find them alienating? Who goes unnoticed in your own life?

3. The Roman poet Terence wrote: "I am a human being; nothing human is alien to me." Could you say this of yourself?

4. Many people have observed a loss of a sense of community in our country. One observer said that it began with central heating – when everyone could go to their private room rather than gathering around the one hearth. How would you account for this shift away from community?

5. Do you have examples from your own life of being "saved" by people who have noticed your plight and attended you through it?

Final prayer and blessing

Almighty and merciful God,
whose Son became a refugee
and had no place to call his own:
look with mercy on those who
are fleeing from danger and violence,
all those who are homeless and hungry.

Bless those who work to bring them relief;
inspire generosity and compassion in all our hearts;
guide the churches and the nations towards that day
when all will rejoice in your kingdom,
a kingdom of justice and of peace,
through Jesus Christ our Lord.
Amen.

May the Lord of all mercies
gift us with his grace
that we might, through all our days,
attend those who look to us
for help and understanding.
May we bless the broken body of Christ
in heeding the needs of our brothers and sisters.
Amen.

Investing in another's greatness

Second week in Advent

Investing in another's greatness

John, the wild man

Moving on

When we look back at our lives, we can probably remember significant people who played a key role in helping us to grow up and choose which paths to take in life. These were the people of affirmation – family, friends, teachers – who encouraged us to believe in ourselves, to take a risk, to make a brave choice about how to make our mark on the world. They invested their time in us and shared their hope that we would amount to something. They might have said to us, "Have you ever thought of becoming…?" or "Why don't you try…?" or "Go on, you can do it!" Sometimes we are introduced to new possibility and a new future by others' stubborn belief in us; we are egged on by those who are neither captivated by their own self-importance nor alarmed at the growing talent of others.

From time to time we are open to change because we experience a lingering dissatisfaction with what we're currently doing, the way our life is moving. We feel that what we're doing, however worthwhile, is somehow not enough. Rather than passively accept this dissatisfaction as part of life, as something that has to be endured, we see it as a signal to move on. We interpret our experience as a sign that

we should look elsewhere, try something different, be open to new opportunity. When this happens our dissatisfaction becomes a positive experience: it leads us to look beyond the boundaries of our own life, to dream of other roads that could be taken.

Sometimes new possibilities open up for us when we see someone doing something we admire and we secretly wonder if our life could go in a similar direction. We feel attracted, drawn in. Is this a call, we wonder, to a new way of life? This fascination is related to how people actually live; it becomes fired by interest not only in what the other person does but in the way that individual relates and looks at life. This fascination is drawn by another person's way of being human, the other person's way of being alive.

Of course we can be fascinated by someone's way of life but have no desire to be engaged in it; we remain observers, unclaimed by what we experience. What we witness is out there to be admired and applauded, but it does not call out to us, it does not have our name written on it. What we see and hear might appear attractive, but it makes no further claim on our attention

or our lives. This is not unlike seeing a play or a film that is inspiring and enjoyable at the time but then is quickly forgotten. A month later we can hardly remember the characters or the plot. Someone or something can momentarily fascinate us, but the experience can fail to leave any lasting impression: life continues as usual.

Sometimes our fascination moves to desire. Sometimes the other captivates our imagination and forces us to pause, to stop what we are doing: we reflect; we want to pursue this experience; we want to claim it in our own lives. When we feel that desire we become apprentices and try to attach ourselves to the person who inspired us. We want to make the original experience a part of our lives. What we have seen and heard is no longer something to admire from a distance – it is now something to participate in, a new life that we want a share in ourselves. We do not walk away or go home; we want to follow what we find compelling.

While some people fascinate us in life and others encourage us, there are also those whose peculiar gift is for diminishment, experts in the destructive word. Having a slender hold on their own dignity, they feel demeaned by the success of others: they pout rather than applaud. These are the kind of people who insist that we will never amount to much, that we are God's mobile mistake, or that we will be a burden on society until a month after

we die. These people belong to what I call the "Nazareth syndrome" – those who want to keep people tied down to their original neighbourhood, to remain within the confines of settled connections, to stay put and forever stagnate, thus proving a threat to nobody.

When people from obscure backgrounds suddenly emerge as important public figures, journalists and television crews often seek out the family and neighbours to discover what they think of the local hero or heroine. Mixed impressions are usually given: delight is shown, congratulations are forthcoming, surprise is admitted, polite disbelief is registered, and sometimes resentment is uncovered. Some neighbours, afraid of admitting their surprise, will declare confidently that they saw it all coming: if they didn't spot it first, it isn't worth knowing. Others are reluctant to acknowledge that anything great could emerge from their postcode; guided by their small-mindedness, they urge caution and hint that nothing much will come of all the hoo-ha.

After his time with John the Baptist, Jesus returns to his own village of Nazareth and teaches in the local synagogue, provoking astonishment from the local townspeople at his performance. Jesus left the town as a carpenter; he now returns as a prophet, eager to share his teaching. Clearly, something has happened to him since he last left home. The neighbours wonder at the origin of Jesus' teaching and the nature of his wisdom, as well as the miracles that are done through him. Questions bubble up: "Where did he get all this? What is this wisdom that has been granted to him? Who does he think he is?"

From the unanswered questions about Jesus' wisdom, the neighbours move to more familiar territory and focus on what they do know about their neighbour. Whatever their wonder, they are not going to allow Jesus' new wisdom to interfere with their memory of him. While their new experience collides with their memory of Jesus, it will be their memory that wins out.

Faced with Jesus' obvious ability, the neighbours support each other in a chorus of distractions. Irrelevant issues are solemnly brought to the centre of attention: the job Jesus worked at, his mother, his

Journey · Preparing · Investing · Adjusting · Welcoming · Celebrating

pedigree, the presence of his brothers and sisters. Of course, the neighbours have a vested interest in focusing on who Jesus was rather than the Jesus who confronts them now: it's easier, after all, having a carpenter around the shop than a prophet loose in the town. So, once a carpenter, always a carpenter. Memory proves to be a useful fiction: it keeps Jesus at the level where they can handle him safely.

Mark summarises the reaction of the Nazareth community to their upstart neighbour: "And they took offence at him" (Mark 6:3). For them, the weight of ordinariness about the Jesus they knew cancels out his new wisdom and works. Nothing kills like frozen familiarity.

How does Jesus react to the locals' pettiness? While he is clearly distressed, he refuses to make their meanness the measure of his performance or allow them to write his script. He confronts them and says:

"Prophets are not without honour, except in their home town, and among their own kin, and in their own house."
(Mark 6:4)

This is a hard saying about his situation, not a general philosophical maxim. In Mark's account Jesus is rejected by his own relations and by those in his own house. No one protests on Jesus' behalf; no one voices support for who he has become: he is on his own. Mark has already told us that Jesus' relatives believe him to be out of his mind (Mark 3:21): now the rejection seems to be complete.

Jesus' experience of rejection in Nazareth renders him powerless to do any miracle among his own people. This is an extraordinary statement about the human Jesus: people's lack of trust limits his ministry. Jesus is profoundly affected by the way people react to him. He is not a robot, programmed for flawless performance, indifferent to all responses. Distrust disables him. So he moves elsewhere, refusing to be enslaved by his inability to reach his own people. And he never returns to Nazareth again. Clearly his own folk preferred the Jesus they knew to the one who emerges after his time with John the Baptist. It is John the Baptist who stands between the hidden life of Jesus and his public ministry.

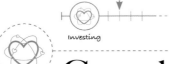

Investing

Gospel text: Mark 1:1-9

The beginning of the good news of Jesus Christ, the Son of God.

As it is written in the book of the prophet Isaiah:

"See, I am sending my messenger ahead of you,
who will prepare your way;
the voice of one crying out in the wilderness:
'Prepare the way of the Lord,
make his paths straight'",

John the baptizer appeared in the wilderness, proclaiming a baptism of repentance for the forgiveness of sins. And people from the whole Judean countryside and all the people of Jerusalem were going out to him, and were baptized by him in the river Jordan, confessing their sins. Now John was clothed with camel's hair, with a leather belt around his waist, and he ate locusts and wild honey. He proclaimed, "The one who is more powerful than I is coming after me; I am not worthy to kneel down and untie the thong of his sandals. I have baptized you with water; but he will baptize you with the Holy Spirit."

In those days Jesus came from Nazareth in Galilee and was baptized by John in the Jordan.

Investing

Reflecting on the Gospel story

Beginning with John

If Advent celebrates new beginnings, it is not surprising to see how quickly the figure of John the Baptist enters the liturgical scene. There is a fixed memory from the tradition that before you tell the story of Jesus you must first speak of the story of John: Jesus' beginning is celebrated in the wider context of the story of John the Baptist, the great reformer who cried out that a new time was approaching and that people should prepare for the coming of someone greater. It is interesting to see how swiftly John the Baptist makes his appearance in the Gospels:

- *Mark's Gospel* opens with the adult John the Baptist preaching and baptising in the wilderness of Judea; then Jesus leaves home in Galilee and travels south to see John by his chosen place of ministry on the banks of the river Jordan.

- *Matthew's Gospel*, after celebrating the birth story of Jesus, opens the story of the public ministry with the revivalist preaching of John. Not only do the people of Jerusalem and Judea make their way to John, but Jesus arrives to be baptised.

- *Luke's Gospel* opens, in the Temple, with the wondrous annunciation of the birth of John the Baptist and carefully parallels the beginning of John's story (annunciation, birth, visitors, circumcision) with the beginning of Jesus' story.

- *John's Gospel* begins before creation and history to celebrate that the Word was with God and was God. The evangelist then interrupts his meditation on eternity by celebrating the unique role of John as a man sent by God to witness to the light of all peoples.

Apart from Matthew's Gospel, all the Gospels introduce John the Baptist at the beginning as a key figure in the Jesus story. The unique place that John enjoys in the written Gospels is reflected in two speeches of Peter from the Acts of the Apostles, reflecting the preaching of the early Church. In the first speech, as they seek to choose a replacement for Judas, Peter establishes the basic criterion for being numbered among the twelve apostles; in the second speech Peter is summarising the Jesus story in the house of Cornelius:

Journey — Preparing — Investing — Adjusting — Welcoming — Celebrating

"So one of the men who have accompanied us throughout the time that the Lord Jesus went in and out among us, beginning from the baptism of John until the day when he was taken up from us – one of these must become a witness with us to his resurrection."
(Acts 1:21-22)

"You know the message [God] sent to the people of Israel, preaching peace by Jesus Christ – he is Lord of all. That message spread throughout Judea, beginning in Galilee after the baptism that John announced."
(Acts 10:36-37)

Peter dates the beginning of the Jesus story not by reference to his birth in Bethlehem but by his emergence from obscurity alongside the figure of John the Baptist. Although Luke is writing these passages, he has chosen a different beginning in his own Gospel – the story of two annunciations, of the births of John and Jesus – which suggests that in Acts Luke is recalling the *earlier* preached boundaries of the Jesus story, from the time of John the Baptist to the return of Jesus in glory; we see the earlier boundary maintained by Mark in the beginning of his Gospel. Peter's assertion makes one thing clear: in a world of uncertainties one thing is certain – Jesus begins after John.

The Gospel witness

John the Baptist is the independent prophetic force that stands between the hidden life of Jesus and his public ministry. Jesus does not begin alone; none of us does. Although Mark reports that John's ministry attracts people from Judea and Jerusalem, the evangelist says nothing about people from Galilee being similarly attracted. Movements popular in the south of a country are not necessarily popular in the north, yet Jesus the Galilean makes the long journey south, which would have taken around four days. Like many other people, he is attracted by the person and preaching of John the Baptist; like many of his contemporaries, he submits to John's baptism of repentance for the forgiveness of sins. After his association with John, Jesus' life takes a dramatic turn. He follows John in the prophetic vocation and reinterprets the message of his mentor.

The four Gospels have their own way of limiting the embarrassing memory of Jesus being baptised by John the Baptist, not least by not showing it in the narrative. What we as readers expect to see is John baptising

Jesus, which is a baptism in water: what we actually see is the Holy Spirit baptising Jesus, and we hear not the voice of John but the voice of God, proclaiming the identity of Jesus.

In Nicolas Poussin's painting *The Sacrament of Baptism*, the artist depicts both scenes. In the centre of the canvas Poussin shows what none of the Gospels does: John baptising Jesus with water.

Journey — Preparing — Investing — Adjusting — Welcoming — Celebrating

The people immediately surrounding the two principal figures, including the artist in black, observe Jesus submitting to John's baptism. As we go further out from the centre, we notice that the observers are no longer looking at John's baptism but at the Spirit's baptism, symbolised by the descent of the dove. In the three Gospel accounts of the baptism, we join the onlookers at the edge of Poussin's painting, witnessing the anointing of Jesus in the power of the Spirit and the revelation of God in announcing Jesus' unique identity. Through this account it is clear that Jesus is superior to John. As John P. Meier argues:

"The theophany does not mirror some inner experience Jesus had at the time; it mirrors the desire of the first-generation Christian church to define Jesus as soon as the primitive Gospel story begins – all the more so because this definition was needed to counter the impression of Jesus' subordination to John, implicit in the tradition of the former being baptized by the latter."[1]

By the time the Gospels are written, John is domesticated within the Christian story and his role is defined simply as a forerunner of Jesus. But John's independent ministry among the people, the moral authority he exercised and the respect he commanded, all still linger in the Gospel tradition. As Joan Taylor notes:

"Since mention of John the Baptist in the New Testament is obviously overlaid with a developing insistence on Jesus' superiority, we can suppose that the issue of John himself was a problem for the early Church. Clearly John was not a nobody in his time, and the Gospels accord him respect. However, John was not permitted too much respect; people had to know his place... most often 'the interpretation aims at neutralizing the Baptist's independence to make him safe for Christianity'."[2]

John's place is assured at the beginning of the Gospel as the nomadic prophet who attracted Jesus from his settled life in Nazareth. Jesus' beginning was not a solitary event in a landscape empty of people. Like many others, Jesus was attracted by John's reputation and was moved to journey to see this fiery reformer who spoke the word of God with authority. And after he saw John, Jesus' life was to take a new direction.

A picture emerges of John as a charismatic leader whose great popularity among the

[1] J.P. Meier, *A Marginal Jew: Rethinking the Historical Jesus*, Vol. 2 (New York: Doubleday, 1994), 107.
[2] J. Taylor, *John the Baptist within Second Temple Judaism* (London: SPCK, 1997), 5.

people is exercised apart from Jesus. His ministry begins before Jesus, and when John dies he leaves behind him a religious following that exists independently of Christianity. John's ministry dominates the beginning of the Gospel, and the fact that Jesus submits to John's baptism clearly indicates that Jesus accepted the Baptist's message calling Israel to repentance, just as he later criticises the leaders for not believing in John (Matthew 21:32).

This radical prophet who erupts onstage before the beginning of Jesus' ministry has a number of particular qualities that make him stand out long after people might suppose his memory would have faded from Christianity:

• John is a threshold figure, marking the boundary between the Old Testament and the New. He represents the past as a figure belonging to the time of the Law and the prophets, but he also represents what is new, calling for a fresh start and heralding the approaching time which comes as a fulfilment of ancient dreams and promises. He is not unlike the figure of Janus, typically depicted, as in a bust from the Vatican Museum, having two

heads, facing in opposite directions: the one who looked to both the past and the future, symbolising change and transition.

- As an independent prophet, John does not owe his authority to being commissioned or contracted by any religious authority. He owes nobody and is tied to no institution. No one in authority, therefore, can dismiss him: since he has not been appointed, he cannot be "disappointed" – only terminated. His authority is charismatic rather than institutional.

- John displays no discernible respect for religious hierarchy and he appears alienated from institutional religion. He emerges in some ways as a peculiarly modern figure – a person who has no automatic respect for authority, civil or religious. He dismisses the chief priests as a brood of vipers and the aristocratic Herod Antipas, the ruler of Galilee and Perea, as a moral degenerate.

- John's natural sanctuary is the wilderness, not the Temple; his theatre of ministry is not sacred space but out of doors, in ordinary space, where he can be reached by any person. His chosen ritual act – baptism – centres on the waters of the river Jordan, not around the priestly altar of sacrifice. His baptism, unlike the regular self-cleansing rituals that required good Jews to wash and then wait for a defined period, is administered by him in the river and is offered only once.

- Working outside sacred space, John attracts a panorama of rejects from the outskirts of society that would never attend the Temple – prostitutes, tax collectors and mercenary soldiers – holding out to them the real possibility of change. According to Luke, different groups of people approach John to seek guidance for their life and ask the question: "What should we do?" (Luke 3:10-14), receiving straightforward answers. In today's language we might say that John had a reputation for being a popular spiritual director not given to indirect counselling techniques.

- John's alienation from normal society is underscored by his ascetic lifestyle in an uninhabited place, his Bedouin dress of animal skin and his peculiar diet of locusts and wild honey.

• As John dies at the hands of a hesitant king – even though Herod knows him to be "a righteous and holy man" (Mark 6:20) – so Jesus will die at the hands of an ambivalent governor who asks, "Why, what evil has he done?" (Mark 15:14). The career of both these resolute men will reach a climax in their execution at the hands of vacillating civil authorities. To know of John is to know in advance of Jesus.

The composite picture of John and his ministry that emerges from the first three Gospels seems to set a stage of conflict, one that Jesus will enter on the side of John.

the holy city of Jerusalem	versus	the wilderness
the Temple (sacrifice)	versus	the river Jordan (baptism)
the institutional	versus	the charismatic
the priestly (sacrifice)	versus	the prophetic (word of God)
the temporal power	versus	the religious critic
the aristocracy	versus	the marginalised
the settled	versus	the nomadic

It's worth noting that this stage of conflict is already established before Jesus begins his ministry. When Jesus leaves home and walks onto the stage of the Gospel, he chooses to stand beside the independent wild man of the wilderness, not the established sacrificial system of the Temple, an option that will soon alienate him from institutional religion. That is why it is worth recalling what all the Gospels note: *Jesus begins after John.*

John and Jesus

There are clear similarities between John and Jesus and also marked differences. The Gospels tend to separate their ministries, to avoid confusion, so that these two giants are not seen on the stage together: "Now after John was arrested, Jesus came to Galilee, proclaiming the good news of God" (Mark 1:14). While Mark notes that the beginning of Jesus' ministry follows on the arrest of John, Luke goes even further and has John offstage, securely locked up in prison, before the account of Jesus' baptism (Luke 3:19-20).

The Fourth Gospel does not share this nervousness about John and Jesus ministering together, not least because the evangelist uses his prologue to clarify the

differences between *Logos* and *anthropos*, between the *Word* who was God and the *man* sent by God as witness. The evangelist introduces John in his prologue as the one who was not the light but was sent to give testimony to the light, a role he fulfils when he acts as the first witness in the Gospel and identifies Jesus as the Lamb of God (John 1:29). John then openly asserts: "I myself have seen and have testified that this is the Son of God" (John 1:34). This portrait of John is reflected in Leonardo da Vinci's famous depiction of John the Baptist – his smile not unlike the enigmatic smile of the Mona Lisa – pointing heavenwards with his right index finger, witnessing to the origin of the chosen one.

In John's Gospel we see something we don't even detect from the earlier Gospels: a time before the arrest of John where we see Jesus and the disciples ministering and baptising in Judea while John baptises in the more difficult territory of Samaria (John 4:1-4). And when Jesus arrives in Samaria he quickly acknowledges the earlier work of John when he says to his disciples: "I sent you to reap that for which you did not labour. Others have laboured, and you have entered into their labour" (John 4:38).

We cannot be certain how long Jesus spent with John; we do know, however, that following the death of John, when Jesus becomes well known in his prophetic career, there is a popular perception that these two men are so close that it is difficult to tell them apart. When Jesus asks his disciples the risky question who the crowds think he is, the first guess is that he is John come back to life, an impression that is confirmed by Herod Antipas (Mark 6:14-16). That perception seems to reflect an early stage in Jesus' ministry, where the likenesses between the two men are paramount in people's minds.

There is a later stage in the Gospel tradition when people begin to notice marked differences between the ministry of Jesus and John. There is a common expectation that Jesus and his disciples will follow John's ascetic tradition – one that is characterised by prayer and fasting – and, interestingly, one of Jesus' disciples asks him to teach them to pray, "as John taught his disciples" (Luke 11:1). That expectation that Jesus will follow John gives way to people's puzzlement at Jesus' divergence: "Then they said to him, 'John's disciples, like the disciples of the Pharisees, frequently fast and pray, but your disciples eat and drink'" (Luke 5:33). Jesus is now seen to do things that John never did – eating and drinking with those who live beyond the boundaries of religious approval, a key difference that is promoted by Jesus himself:

> "For John the Baptist has come eating no bread and drinking no wine, and you say, 'He has a demon'; the Son of Man has come eating and drinking, and you say, 'Look, a glutton and a drunkard, a friend of tax-collectors and sinners!'"
> (Luke 7:33-34)

Jesus does not minister in the wilderness, attracting crowds from the city and countryside who journey out to listen to his message; rather, Jesus goes in the opposite direction in taking the initiative to reach out to people where they are, travelling to their towns and villages, preaching in the synagogues, entering their houses, and eating at table. Not only does Jesus differ from John in the ministry of table-fellowship, but whereas there is no tradition that John's ministry included healing or exorcism, these are constants in the ministry of Jesus. While both John and Jesus preached the coming of the kingdom of God, that reality is seen as somehow

Journey — Preparing — Investing — Adjusting — Welcoming — Celebrating

present in Jesus' ministry: "But if it is through the finger of God that I cast out the demons, then the kingdom of God has come to you" (Luke 11:20).

For all the similarities and differences between John and Jesus, it is extraordinary how the memory of John is fixed and honoured in the Christian tradition. While Jesus overshadowed John, the Baptist's presence is stubbornly venerated in the Jesus story. John might be remembered not least because he provoked from Jesus the extraordinary estimation of his place in human history: "I tell you, among those born of women no one is greater than John" (Luke 7:28). While John may have been unsure of Jesus' identity, sending his disciples to question him, Jesus is sure about John and honours him like no other human being. This provokes an obvious question: what did John do for Jesus to merit such a unique accolade?

After John

In the Gospels the reported retrospective account of Jesus' relatives and neighbours plays an important part in the drama because the voices testify to a view of Jesus that was unremarkable in its expectations and refers back to a time that is outside the purview of the Gospels. In the Gospel narratives there is no Nazareth testimony that one day Jesus' sleeping greatness would emerge, no neighbour's voice welcoming the emergent prophet as someone whose power was foreseen. There is no memory reported of an extraordinary birth that might have heralded an extraordinary life, no hint of angelic choirs once heard, of a reported visit from wise men from the east, or of wholesale slaughter of innocent children by a despotic Herod. The people of Nazareth fasten on to what they actually know about their neighbour Jesus, a view rooted in their own experience:

> "'Is not this the carpenter, the son of Mary and brother of James and Joses and Judas and Simon, and are not his sisters here with us?' And they took offence at him."
> (Mark 6:3)

The people of Nazareth are witnessing a startling and unsettling change that they cannot account for from their own experience and familiarity with Jesus. They see no relationship between the Jesus they think they know and the Jesus now before them, who is acting out of a new identity and direction in life. He has moved away from the traditional double loyalty to religion and family to a new loyalty to the kingdom of God and his new family, whom he defines not by blood relations but by acceptance of the word of God.

The voice of Jesus' neighbours is important because it testifies to the dramatic change that Jesus has made since he left home and spent time with John the Baptist. The townspeople have no trouble accepting the Jesus they knew – before he went to see John the Baptist. And they refuse to accept the Jesus who now presents himself in the role of a prophet and teacher.

How John the Baptist stands at the turning point of Jesus' life can be seen in the following way:

Jesus before John		Jesus after John
"This is Joseph's son"	identity	prophet / teacher
woodworker in hill village of Nazareth	direction of life	wandering mission to lost sheep of the house of Israel
loyalty to Judaism and to family	outlook	kingdom of God and new family

The change happened while Jesus was with John, and for the remainder of his ministry and life Jesus lives out that deliberate reordering of his life. The influence of John the Baptist on Jesus is recognised reluctantly; I have listed a number of instances below.

Like John, Jesus:

- remained unmarried and followed a calling in the prophetic tradition;
- preached out of doors;
- remained independent of other religious groups;
- proclaimed, "Repent, for the kingdom of heaven is close at hand";
- gathered his own disciples;
- baptised with water;
- confronted religious authorities;
- opened up new life for tax collectors, prostitutes, etc.;
- questioned the special place of Israel, rejecting nationalism;
- was rejected by Pharisees and leaders;
- rejected the self-righteous, and accepted notorious sinners;
- gave disciples prayer to characterise them;
- was believed to be the Messiah;
- was handed over and executed by civil powers;
- was believed to be risen from the dead.

While Jesus seems to begin in the shadow of John the Baptist – with many people believing that he is John risen from the dead – the time comes when Jesus diverges from John and initiates a new way of relating to God and neighbour. When any of us begin to teach, we begin in the shadow of our mentors, because we were first learners and disciples before we became teachers and leaders. There is nothing strange about this emergence: it is the normal pattern of development and growth. But we look back with profound gratitude to our teachers and mentors, especially those who believed not only that we would become great one day, but that we would surpass them.

Investing

Questions for reflection

1. Imagine yourself to be a neighbour of Jesus in the first century, living in the small town of Nazareth, which has a population of around one hundred and fifty people. Everyone knows everyone else; there are not many secrets. Jesus the carpenter leaves home for some time, and when he returns he unexpectedly presents himself in the local synagogue as a prophet and teacher, proclaiming with authority that the ancient prophecy of Isaiah is being fulfilled even as he speaks. How do you think you would react?

2. When you look back at the time of your own formation, how many teachers can you remember with gratitude? When you look back over the span of your life, who were the people who encouraged you to grow, to spread your wings, to make something of yourself?

3. Who would you be without the people who believed in you?

4. If you were a teacher, would you feel threatened by a very bright student in your class who had already overtaken you in knowledge and insight?

5. In your own life, who do you encourage, support and mentor?

Journey — Preparing — Investing — Adjusting — Welcoming — Celebrating

Final prayer and blessing

We pray that the Lord in his kindness
will bless all the people who blessed us
with their encouragement and support,
all those who helped us become who we are.

May the good Lord enliven us,
in our turn, to reach out to others,
especially those who need our belief,
those who hunger for our constant support.
May we comfort them in times of misfortune
and rejoice with them in their success.
This we pray through Christ our Lord.
Amen.

May the God and Father of our Lord Jesus Christ
bless us with the gift of faith in his beloved Son,
that we might ever believe and hope in him.

May God be with us in our times of doubt;
may God accompany us in our times of darkness;
may God console us in our times of despair.

In all that we do and say,
may the loving kindness of our God
go out from us as a blessing to others.
Amen.

Adjusting to new directions

Third week in Advent

Adjusting to new directions

Joseph, the quiet man

Where to begin?

In the course of our lives we experience many new beginnings, and it can be interesting to take a little time to review the process of our life story and mark the more significant beginnings we have experienced along the way. There are obvious ones to note: birth, schooling, leaving home, beginning relationships, starting a job, settling into a partnership or single life or marriage, beginning a family, moving to new places, retirement. How much of our life has been advanced by our own choices? How much has been influenced by circumstances not of our choosing?

There can, of course, be new beginnings in disruptive experiences: death of a loved one, divorce, unemployment, exposure of some flaw by the media, being dismissed from our job, and a litany of other external influences that we did not decide on ourselves. Some new beginnings are not of our choosing and are forced upon us by circumstances, but they can have the weight of shaping a future life. Sometimes life is interrupted by unforeseen events, and the interruption prompts a new beginning and a new story.

Often autobiographies and biographies begin at the predictable beginning, usually the birth, and trace the life story through a time sequence, attempting to give some overarching framework to the narrative of a life that might otherwise appear provisional and makeshift. There is a compulsion to find meaning and structure amidst all the varied choices and happenings in the life story, to paint a picture that makes sense to the reader. Some people find this yearning for structure puzzling because they believe that the progress of a life with its myriad and complicated choices defies real explanation: why, they ask, do people feel compelled to construct a performance out of a life that is by definition accidental?

In the biblical narrative, as indeed in most narrative writing, you usually meet people in the middle of things: this is how we meet most people in life – in the middle of things. People enter our lives, as we enter theirs, without much notice or biographical notes, and we learn about their character by observing how they relate to us and others and the world around them; we notice what values they bring to the interaction; we guess how they might be dominated by secret compulsions. When some people make an impact on us, we become

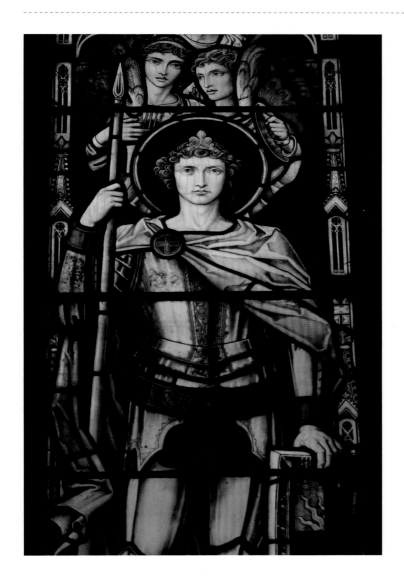

interested in who they are, and we try to understand how and why they choose to do what they do.

We learn about people best by actually relating to them; we learn less by just observing them, by watching how they manage their relationships and their work. When we relate to people we hear the inside story as we listen to their take on life; we get an insight into how they are hurt or haunted by what has already happened in their life; we learn about their hopes and fears, and gradually become aware why they respond to things the way they do. We hear about the delights and the pressures. We worry about how they will face up to new challenges. How will they confront conflicts not of their own making?

If part of our life is lived out in the active voice, where we feel in charge and our verbs define who we are, another part of our life is lived in the passive voice, where unforeseen things happen to us and we have to face or endure the consequences.

If all stories proceed through conflict – there is no story without one – writers usually establish the conflict early in the story. "Once upon a time everyone lived happily ever after" is not a story for the simple reason that there is no conflict. If you watch any film or read any novel, conflict will often appear on the first page or in the first scene. Conflict is friction, tension, opposition: it is the driving force of story, as indeed it is in the narrative of the Gospels. If there is nothing in a story to fight against, nothing to win, nothing to lose, why would anyone bother reading on? If the principal character never struggles, is never tested by adversity, never battles against outside forces, the story goes nowhere.

Conflict is not just essential to the development of a story, it is the essence of every story. What makes a story interesting and engaging is the conflict that stands between the principal characters and their chosen goal. Readers want to become involved in the protagonist's personal battle to achieve a specific goal, and if the writer successfully engages the readers in that struggle they will worry about whether or not the hero or heroine can actually reach the goal. Conflict stimulates that worry. Another way of looking at conflict is to think of it as a barrier: conflict is what stands in the way of the protagonist; it is the force that needs to be overcome if the

story is to reach a successful conclusion. Conflict is when two forces are in opposition to each other.

In a story, as in life, we begin to understand characters by seeing how they respond to conflict. How individuals react to challenging situations defines their character. We respond to how characters deal with conflict because we have to relate to conflict in our own lives: it is part of our everyday living to cope with conflict and endure struggle. Seeing how Jesus in the Gospel narratives faces a variety of conflicts helps us not only to understand his character and values but to gain perspective on our own lives; the same is true as we watch the disciples facing their own tensions.

If we disagree with the choices a character makes when dealing with conflict, like Judas for example, we can form negative opinions about that individual. If we admire the choices characters make, like the women followers who stubbornly stay with Jesus through his crucifixion and death, we admire them more. The way people face conflict evokes our admiration or disapproval; it helps us choose which character to support in the drama of action.

In taking sides we also reveal ourselves to ourselves.

Matthew is alone among the evangelists in choosing Joseph as his principal character in the opening of his Gospel. The character of Joseph – who appears only in the infancy narrative – is developed by showing how he faces conflict in his life and how he manages to respond to what is asked of him by God. There is no biographical introduction to Joseph, no information about his family or background: we see him onstage for the first time facing a huge challenge in life, one that is clearly not of his own making.

Adjusting

Gospel text: Matthew 1:18-25

Now the birth of Jesus the Messiah took place in this way. When his mother Mary had been engaged to Joseph, but before they lived together, she was found to be with child from the Holy Spirit.

Her husband Joseph, being a righteous man and unwilling to expose her to public disgrace, planned to dismiss her quietly. But just when he had resolved to do this, an angel of the Lord appeared to him in a dream and said, "Joseph, son of David, do not be afraid to take Mary as your wife, for the child conceived in her is from the Holy Spirit. She will bear a son, and you are to name him Jesus, for he will save his people from their sins."

All this took place to fulfil what the Lord had spoken through the prophet:

"Look, the virgin shall conceive and bear
   a son,
and they shall name him Emmanuel",

which means "God is with us." When Joseph awoke from sleep, he did as the angel of the Lord commanded him; he took her as his wife, but had no marital relations with her until she had borne a son; and he named him Jesus.

Journey Preparing Investing Adjusting Welcoming Celebrating

Adjusting

Reflecting on the Gospel story

Joseph: a life interrupted

In the Gospel narratives Joseph is the quiet man of Christianity who lives his life offstage while others work through the drama centre stage. We know very little about Joseph: he is never mentioned by name in the earliest Gospel, Mark's, nor in the reported preaching of the early Church; but while he is alluded to, in passing, by Luke and John, Matthew brings him centre stage during the birth narrative and we are invited to see the beginning of Jesus' life through the challenges that Joseph faces. Matthew's sequence of the Joseph story can be read through watching Joseph face six interruptions in his life. (In my book *Awakening to Yourself: Reflecting with Paintings Volume 2*, I explored the drama of Joseph through imagining him blogging on the internet about the challenges happening in his life.)[1]

First interruption

In Matthew's Gospel Joseph shares similarities with the ancient patriarch Joseph, who was characterised by his dreams and saved the life of his family by bringing them to the land of Egypt. When Matthew's Joseph first appears, he is portrayed as having already entered into the formal contract of betrothal to Mary;

the second part of the contract, living together, has yet to take place. Although the couple are not sharing bed and board, Matthew refers to Joseph as Mary's husband (Matthew 1:19).

The new husband discovers the shocking news – we are not told how – that his wife is pregnant outside their relationship: in a world of uncertainties he knows one thing for sure, that he is not the father. While we the readers are told by the evangelist how this came to be, Joseph remains in the dark. We the readers are wiser than the protagonist in this story. As Raymond Brown comments:

> "The fact that the child was conceived through the Holy Spirit is not part of the narrative flow here; rather the news comes to the dramatis personae from an angel's revelation... But Matthew wants the readers to know more than do the characters in the story, so that the reader will not entertain for a moment the suspicion that grows in Joseph's mind."[2]

Joseph, a righteous man, is in personal anguish at this aching discovery. What to do? How do you manage such an early disaster in a marriage and, as much as possible, save the face of all parties?

Journey   Preparing   Investing   Adjusting   Welcoming   Celebrating

Joseph's immediate resolve is to divorce Mary – a decision that is introduced by noting that Joseph is a just man, who would want to observe the Law, particularly with regard to sexual relations (see Deuteronomy 22:13-27; 24:1). He resolves not to take Mary to court to face a public inquiry before the rigour of the Law, but to divorce her quietly, in the presence of select witnesses, thus avoiding a public spectacle. Though it would be impossible to keep this divorce a secret in a small town – the resultant shame would surely follow – Joseph believes that, given the options, his chosen way is the most humane and the kindest way to proceed.

Second interruption

Certain that his decision is the right one, Joseph goes to bed, no doubt determined to act on his resolution in the morning. His life is interrupted for a second time, however, this time by the appearance of an angel in his dream who first counsels him not to be afraid and then makes the startling annunciation:

> "Joseph, son of David, do not be afraid to take Mary as your wife, for the child conceived in her is from the Holy Spirit. She will bear a son, and you are to name him Jesus, for he will save his people from their sins."
> (Matthew 1:20-21)

Joseph now learns from the angel what we as readers have already been told by the evangelist: that the child is conceived by the Holy Spirit. In the light of this revelation, will Joseph follow his natural instinct, to divorce Mary, or will he pursue the stuff of dreams? Will he separate himself from Mary and carve out a new life for himself, or take her to his home in Bethlehem, confirming her as his wife? Will he give the name to this child, as commanded in the dream, thus becoming the child's legal father? Or will the delicate revelation in the dark of night fade in the gathering glow of the morning light?

In W.H. Auden's poem "A Christmas Oratorio", there is a section entitled "The Temptation of St Joseph" in which a chorus offstage repeatedly sows doubt in Joseph's mind. They say:

> "Joseph, you have heard
> What Mary says occurred;
> Yes, it may be so.
> Is it likely? No.

[1] D. McBride, *Awakening to Yourself: Reflecting with Paintings Volume 2* (Chawton: Redemptorist Publications, 2009), 9-39.
[2] R. Brown, *The Birth of the Messiah* (London: Geoffrey Chapman, 1993), 24.

Mary may be pure,
But, Joseph, are you sure?
How is one to tell?
Suppose, for instance... Well...

Maybe, maybe not.
But, Joseph, you know what
Your world, of course, will say
About you anyway."[3]

What voices will Joseph listen to? Will he continue to listen to his own voice or will he listen to the voice of the angel announcing that God is doing new things, and that these new plans are counting on Joseph for his cooperation and blessing?

Matthew retains the focus on Joseph, not least perhaps because Joseph represents all those just Jews who, at the time of the Gospel's writing, are being asked to accept the new things God is doing in Jesus: they are being invited to go against their inclinations and exclusive veneration of the tradition and see God's providence in new events that, at first, seem irregular and extraordinary. Matthew's belief is firm: God has not only spoken through tradition but is speaking in new events that are happening in the present tense. In this case

there is no point in Joseph consulting the sacred tradition: there is no precedent of a virgin birth in the Hebrew scriptures.

When Joseph wakes up he decides to follow his dream, not his instincts, a decision that will change his life for ever. Matthew's brief narrative of this upright Jewish man, who comes to welcome the unexpected and adjust his life to God's revelation, stands in dramatic contrast to the Jewish religious authorities in Jerusalem who, when they are unexpectedly confronted with magi seeking the address of the king of the Jews and themselves uncover the address as revealed in scripture (Matthew 2:5-6), do not follow the revelation but leave it unheeded on the scroll on which they found it. Joseph is Matthew's outstanding Jewish hero in his infancy narrative. For the writer, Joseph's real story begins in conflict, in a life interrupted by the unexpected: while in most cultures wives have to adjust to their husband's plans, Joseph is startled by a contrary demand, which he learns to accept as a new beginning.

In Matthew's Gospel it seems paradoxical that the birth of Jesus is mentioned, in passing, as part of the drama of Joseph:

"When Joseph awoke from sleep, he did as the angel of the Lord commanded him; he took her as his wife, but had no marital relations with her until she had borne a son; and he named him Jesus." (Matthew 1:24-25)

The birth of Jesus is passed over without any narrative detail. The attention stays stubbornly on Joseph, who is seen to fulfil the double command of the angel by taking Mary home and, after the birth, naming the child. In Matthew's account Jesus is born at home in Bethlehem; in Luke's account Joseph comes from Nazareth with Mary south to Bethlehem for the enrolment, where Jesus is born in a stable and laid in a manger (Luke 2:6-7). While Matthew has to move his story from Bethlehem to Nazareth, Luke has the opposite challenge in moving his story from Nazareth to Bethlehem. In both cases, however, Bethlehem is celebrated as the place of Jesus' birth: as the home of David and the place of his anointing, there is no more appropriate place for the birth of the one who has been introduced in Matthew's Gospel as "son of David" (Matthew 1:1).

3 W.H. Auden, *Collected Longer Poems* (New York: Vintage, 1975), 149-150.

Third interruption

Not only the life of Joseph but the life of the new family is interrupted by the unannounced arrival of a group of exotic characters from the east, an interruption that will prove fatal for the life of the town. While this visit will have the effect of making this family exiles and refugees, it will also have catastrophic consequences for all the other local families with newborn male children.

While the birth is anticipated in the annunciation to Joseph, it is mentioned as being already over in the story of the magi. Although Joseph enjoyed the focus of attention in the previous story, he is not even mentioned in this story; Mary's name is mentioned, but she plays a subsidiary role. The real focus is on two dramatically different responses to the birth of Jesus: one of acceptance, illustrated by the Gentiles – the magi who come from the east and worship the true king of the Jews; the other of rejection, shown by the Jewish authorities – King Herod, the chief priests and the scribes.

This story will act as an overture not only to the main body of the Gospel but also to the experience of Matthew's church,

announcing the broad themes of Gentile acceptance and the Jewish authorities' rejection of Jesus. The first to pay homage to Jesus are Gentiles from the east, illustrating Jesus' later promise: "I tell you, many will come from east and west and will eat with Abraham and Isaac and Jacob in the kingdom of heaven" (Matthew 8:11).

The country of origin of the mysterious magi is not specified – traditional guesses focus on three places: Arabia, Babylon or Persia. (The name *magoi* was originally associated with the Medes and Persians. When Emperor Justinian rebuilt the Church of the Nativity at Bethlehem, the façade was redecorated with images of the magi. When the Persians attacked the Holy Land in AD 614, they did not destroy the basilica at Bethlehem when they saw the magi depicted in the familiar dress of their own people.) Neither is their number given – it is popularly presumed to be three from the count of their gifts, although eastern tradition numbers them as twelve. Their function, however, is clear in Matthew's narrative: they represent the spiritual elite of the Gentile world, the ancestors of all foreigners who will find their true destination in Jesus. If Abraham was the "ancestor of a multitude of nations"

(Genesis 17:5), this "son of Abraham" (Matthew 1:1) is seen at his birth as the one in whom all nations are blessed.

It was a common motif in the ancient world that a new star marked the birth of a ruler: the astrological sign in Matthew's narrative, a sign of nature, moves the magi to see the significance of the Davidic star. Their instinct is not to sit and discuss this new phenomenon but to follow it, to welcome this new heavenly sign as their teacher. The star, however, does not by itself lead the Gentile seekers to the place of the birth: the Gentiles must first go to the Jews and learn from them, through a revelation in the scriptures, the truth of God's providential plan. It will be through a combination of sources – a sign from nature and God's revelation contained in the Jewish scriptures – that the magi will reach their destination in Jesus.

So it is in Matthew's narrative that the star does not lead the magi directly to Bethlehem, but instead their journey takes them five miles north to the city of Jerusalem, where they enjoy ready access to King Herod and his court. The magi are not seen to pay homage to King Herod or offer him gifts, in dramatic contrast to their later act of prostrating themselves in worship before the infant king of the Jews and presenting him with royal gifts. Instead, the magi pragmatically move to business at hand and make no secret of why they have come, to offer homage to the infant king of the Jews: their naive disclosure will cause chaos in the near future. On hearing the news, the establishment of Judea gathers in an aristocratic huddle of discontent. The outsiders have unsettled the institution: the scene is set for conflict.

It may not appear to be a particularly wise move to tell the reigning king of the Jews that you are looking for the new one! Herod is perturbed – a predictable reaction in the circumstances, given that his throne seems to be in immediate danger – and his anxiety is shared by the whole city of Jerusalem. Matthew appears to illustrate, as he will do later in his passion narrative, official Judaism united in opposition to Jesus.

In response to the startling revelation, Herod calls together the wise men of Judea – the chief priests and the scribes – to discover the birthplace of the Messiah. In uncovering the secret from the scriptures, the future enemies of Jesus now ironically testify to the birth of Jesus and his Messiahship: the shepherd of Israel is to be born in Bethlehem, the city from which another shepherd, King David, came and where he was anointed.

Herod now summons the magi and sees them secretly, to learn the exact date on which the star appeared; here Matthew prepares for Herod's command to kill all male children two years old and under, "according to the time that he had learned from the wise men" (Matthew 2:16). Having discovered the secret from the Jewish wise men about the place of the birth, and having discovered the secret from the Gentile wise men of the time of the star's rising, Herod now commands the magi to find out everything about the child, return and report all to him, so that he can offer this child king due homage.

Herod's assumption that the magi would become his informants and accomplices seems out of character for such a cunning king: it does not seem beyond the wit of Herod to send spies to follow the magi the five miles to Bethlehem; otherwise, it would hardly be difficult to identify the address of a house in a small Judean town, one that is marked by the arrival of

a caravan of exotic foreigners, carrying treasures from the east, and identified by a star!

As the magi set out south for Bethlehem, to their delight the star appears again as their guide and halts over the place where the child is. Why did the star not lead them here in the first place, without a detour to Jerusalem, thus avoiding the massacre of the innocents? A star halting over a particular address seems unusual. Matthew's star seems less of a celestial phenomenon when it identifies a particular house: if the ancients regarded stars as animate beings, and Jews tended to identify them with angels (Job 38:7), this star functions more like the angelic guide of the exodus, whose function is to bring the expedition "to the place that I have prepared" (Exodus 23:20).

The magi enter the house of Joseph and, on seeing the child with his mother Mary, they wordlessly fall on their knees and do him homage. This child is their real destination, their determined focus, the object of their worship. They open their treasures now and offer their curious gifts to this infant king. Whatever their plans were, a dream instructs them not to return to Herod and so become his accomplices: thus they return to their own country by a different way (Matthew 2:12).

Matthew develops the scene with the care of a master storyteller. He ranges the wise men who follow natural means – a star – against the wise men of Judea who are able to follow their own sign – the scriptures. It is clear from the story that the wise men of Judea have enough information in the scriptures to discover the place where the new Davidic king will be born; but their discovery is useless, for it does not lead them to homage. They are not disposed to act on what has been revealed. By contrast, the pagan strangers, after they have gone as far as they can in following the star, are willing to be instructed in a scripture that is foreign to them. They act on what has been given to them, and their journey leads them to their destination.

Matthew shows how two wisdoms collide: the wisdom of the Jewish institution and the wisdom of the pagan strangers. The wise strangers pass by the institution: their destination is not the palace of the king but a newborn child; their journey's end is not the institution of power but the person of Jesus.

For Matthew, the wise strangers are the vanguard of all peoples who make their own journey to God in Christ. They may have taken a route that seemed curious to a religious establishment that had so many antique maps in its possession; but the Lord draws all sorts of different people to him by all sorts of different routes. The wandering magi were led to God more by natural wonder than by dogmatic instruction, and this has made them symbols of hope for all who struggle to God by strange routes.

Fourth interruption

The magi return by a different route, avoiding Jerusalem, thus leaving Herod to wait on the expected intelligence. These first visitors to Jesus will leave chaos in their wake. They are good people, for sure, but sometimes decent and even saintly people can unknowingly cause upheaval in the lives of others as they make their choices and journey on, unaffected by what they leave behind them. While the magi bring their faith and extravagant gifts, they also bring danger to the house of Joseph and the whole town of Bethlehem.

From the stately scene of gift-giving we move to desperate scenes of flight and murder. After the magi take their leave, Joseph's life is interrupted again by another dream. The family's escape is prompted by the appearance of an angel in Joseph's dream, warning him of Herod's intentions to kill the child, and commanding Joseph to flee to Egypt and stay there until he is alerted that it is safe to return. Herod's power had no sway in Egypt, which had been under direct Roman control since 30 BC, and although the dominant memory of Egypt for the Israelites was as a place of bondage, it also served as a popular place of refuge – for instance, when Solomon heard that Jeroboam was plotting against him, the king condemned him to death, and Jeroboam "fled to Egypt" (1 Kings 11:40), where the Pharaoh granted him political asylum.

In escaping to Egypt, Joseph is again seen to adjust his life to follow his dream, carrying out the angel's command. One of the characteristic elements in the story of the patriarchs is the frequent use of dreams in which they are called upon to face hardship and adversity that will challenge their capacity and commitment: four times Matthew shows how Joseph is diverted through his dreams to take other roads (Matthew 1:20; 2:13. 19. 22). Matthew's portrait of Joseph will remind his readers

of Joseph in the Old Testament, "the man of dreams" who saved his family by bringing them to Egypt: again there is the image of Egypt as refuge. Jesus is seen symbolically to relive the Old Testament story not only of Joseph going to Egypt but also of Israel returning from there in the exodus.

Matthew adds the editorial comment that this happened to fulfil what the Lord had spoken to the prophet: "Out of Egypt I have called my son" (Matthew 2:15; see Hosea 11:1, "When Israel was a child, I loved him, and out of Egypt I called my son"). The quotation originally referred to God's

Journey — Preparing — Investing — Adjusting — Welcoming — Celebrating

calling Israel, God's son, from Egypt at the time of the exodus. Matthew clearly sees Jesus recapitulating the experience of Israel: Jesus is the embodiment of the true Israel. Jesus, like Moses before him, begins his life as a refugee in flight from a wicked king: a comprehensive list of the main points of contact between the two stories is supplied by Dale Allison in his study of Matthew's typology that includes the possibility of a tradition about the virgin birth of Moses.[4]

Outwitted by the wise men, King Herod orders the slaughter of all male children who are two years or younger. Although the massacre of the children is in keeping with Herod's character – he did not hesitate to execute anyone who threatened his throne – there is no independent witness to Matthew's story in extant literature; Josephus, who catalogues the horrors of Herod's reign, makes no mention of it. As the massacre of the children refers back to the persecution of the Israelites in Egypt, so the reference to Rachel and Ramah refers back to the story of the exile.

The three places that are mentioned in Matthew's scriptural quotations – Bethlehem, the city of David; Egypt, the land of the exodus; Ramah, the mourning staging post of the exile – present a geographical microcosm of the history of Israel. That history is now recapitulated in the story of Jesus, one that is celebrated as being not only in theological continuity with the story of Israel but its fulfilment.

Matthew's portrait of the Holy Family is a timeless one, which is part of our present world: a family is uprooted by violence and takes to the road, hunting for a people and a place that will receive them with hospitality and offer them what their home place cannot – security and peace. They are not economic migrants, searching for fresh opportunities, but real refugees, fleeing from harm and the brute force of a tyranny that is accountable to no one.

Fifth interruption

There is no hint in Matthew's narrative how long the Holy Family stayed in Egypt. For the Gentile Christians in Matthew's community, it would be a source of pride that while Jesus' home place in Judea became a place of danger, the place of safety and refuge was a Gentile country, indeed a traditional enemy, that offered them hospitality and protection until it was

[4] See D. Allison, *The New Moses: A Matthean Typology* (Edinburgh: T&T Clark, 1993), 142-146.

safe to return. It is an early sign in Matthew's Gospel: not only are the first worshippers of Jesus Gentile, but Jesus' decreed place of acceptance is in the Gentile world.

Following the death of Herod the Great, Joseph's life is interrupted again as he is instructed through a dream to take a new direction in his life: "Get up, take the child and his mother, and go to the land of Israel, for those who were seeking the child's life are dead" (Matthew 2:20; see Exodus 4:19). Without demur, Joseph follows the command promptly, so that again we see Joseph as the obedient Jew who follows this new word of the Lord, announcing the will of God: "Then Joseph got up, took the child and his mother, and went to the land of Israel" (Matthew 2:21).

Later in Matthew's Gospel Jesus will define his real family: "whoever does the will of my Father in heaven is my brother and sister and mother" (Matthew 12:50). Already we can see that Joseph, acting in obedience to God's word and following God's will, belongs to the real family of Jesus.

Sixth interruption

Joseph naturally starts to head for Judea, presumably to Bethlehem where he has his home, but when he hears – we are not told the source – that Archelaus now rules over that region, he is afraid to go there. His fear is entirely justified by events.

In the final version of his will Herod named Archelaus, his eldest surviving son, as principal heir to his kingdom. Archelaus refrained from using the royal title "king" – one that could be bestowed only by the Emperor Augustus – but was soon faced with demands for the reduction and abolition of taxes, the release of prisoners, and the replacement of the high priest appointed by his father. In order to settle the serious unrest that followed, Archelaus ordered his cavalry into the Temple precincts: they killed three thousand Jews in a bloodthirsty purge (Josephus, *Antiquities* 17.218).

Archelaus sailed to Rome to petition Augustus for his father's throne. During his absence, the civil unrest developed into widespread rebellion. The Roman governor of Syria, Varus, restored order and also gave permission for a Jewish delegation to sail to Rome to oppose the claim of Archelaus: they requested that Judea be annexed and ruled directly from Rome (Josephus, *Antiquities* 17.299-314). Augustus compromised: he divided Herod's property, probably to ensure the future of Herod's dependants and to go some way to satisfy the Jewish delegation that demanded abolition of the monarchy. He awarded the title of ethnarch (leader of a race) to Archelaus, with the territories of Judea, Samaria and Idumea, together with a number of cities, including Jerusalem. Antipas was confirmed as tetrarch (leader of a quarter) of the regions of Galilee and Perea; Philip as tetrarch of the areas north and west of the Sea of Galilee.

Although Archelaus did not gain the title king, it is interesting to note that Josephus calls him "king" – which might be a popular indication of the scope of Archelaus' power. On his return he exacted a cruel revenge on his opponents. Speaking of Archelaus' tyrannical rule, Josephus notes how Archelaus, "remembering past differences, behaved savagely not only towards Jews but also towards the Samaritans" (Josephus, *Jewish War* 2.111). Archelaus remained in office only ten years, until AD 6. Because of Archelaus' stubborn commitment to violence as his principal form of government, Augustus summoned him to Rome, exiled him to Gaul, and appointed a Roman procurator to govern his territories.

Another dream intervenes to divert Joseph from his chosen path, this time instructing him to go to Galilee, a region traditionally known as Galilee of the Gentiles (see Matthew 4:15, quoting Isaiah 8:23 – 9:1). Ruled by Herod Antipas, a full brother of Archelaus, Galilee enjoyed a more peaceful political climate than Judea.

Joseph withdraws (Greek *anachorein*) to the region of Galilee. Matthew tends to use this verb when Jesus leaves a place because of people's unbelief (see Matthew 2:14; 4:12; 12:15; 14:13; 15:21); from it will come, in later Christianity, a technical term for monasticism as a withdrawal from public life into contemplation (anchorite). Joseph settles in a town called Nazareth in fulfilment of the prophetic word: "He will be called a Nazorean" (Matthew 2:23). Although scholars can find no equivalent line in any passage of the Old Testament, Matthew concludes his infancy narrative with the name that will for ever identify the son of David, the son of Abraham, the Son of God: Jesus of Nazareth. Matthew closes

his infancy narrative having effectively moved the family, through the drama of Joseph, from home to exile in Egypt, from exile back to Israel, then north to Galilee, specifically to the town of Nazareth. The psychological and spiritual drama of Joseph covers a large geographical map, the journey concluding by settling Jesus in Nazareth, in place for the beginning of his public ministry.

After these six interruptions, Joseph leaves the stage and we hear no more of him in Matthew's great narrative.

Conclusion

From the outset of the story, Joseph is asked to change and welcome the new things God is doing in his life. All of us have been asked to make changes in our lives, but few of us have been asked to make such dramatic changes as Joseph was. He is the patron saint of all who are expected to adapt and change because of what is going on in other people's lives. The real drama is happening elsewhere and they are being asked to adapt. In most cultures wives are still expected to fit into their husband's plans; if he is moved with the job, the wife and children trail behind him and settle in a new place. Joseph is the opposite: he is

the husband who is being asked to fit into the plans for his wife's life – to say yes, to agree, to accommodate himself into God's plan for her life. Although Matthew gives Joseph centre stage for a brief while, the remainder of his Gospel is silent about his first hero. The attention moves away from Joseph and settles on Jesus until the conclusion of the Gospel.

Joseph has to undergo a reversal of the normal roles in his society: in conception the male presence is essential, so it is rather difficult for a man to accept that in this situation he is surplus to requirements, that he is neither required nor needed. So this gentle dreamer must follow his dreams to plan the life of the Holy Family. He takes Mary home as his wife and recognises Jesus as his son. Jesus will be known as his son, the son of the carpenter. And Jesus will follow in his father's footsteps, up to a point.

Together Joseph and Mary will be the first to love Jesus and the first to teach him. However small a part they play in the Gospel, Mary and Joseph did not have walk-on parts in Jesus' life – they are both essential to his growth and security. Jesus will be schooled in their

love and grow up in its sanctuary. When children want to know what love is, they consult their experience – that is the only book of wisdom available to them. When Jesus becomes an adult, love will become so important to him that he will say that everything else is unimportant beside it. That love he learned first as the child of Mary and Joseph.

It's good to celebrate the generous people who are happy to live in the shadows, nourishing the greatness of others. Maybe we can think of our parents or grandparents, or others in our lives, people who were not hungry for the spotlight but were happy to play their supportive role, content that they were not conspicuous characters in the big drama of life. Jesus' life could not have progressed without these people. Neither could ours.

Adjusting

Questions for reflection

1. In reviewing Matthew's story of Jesus, count how many times Joseph was diverted from his intended path. Does Joseph emerge for you as a weak or a strong character? Why?

2. If you were painting a full portrait of Joseph, would you paint a large lily in his left hand? What would you put in the picture that would reflect your view of Joseph? (As I wrote this I just had an image of Joseph tearing up maps and throwing them onto the wood of the fire!)

3. Looking back at our lives, most of us can detect key moments when life was interrupted and we had to face new challenges. Has your life ever been interrupted to such an extent that the interruption shaped the rest of your life?

4. How many times have you had to adjust your life to fit in with the plans of those close to you? Was it worth it?

5. What new things do you believe God is doing today, especially things that are not part of the sacred tradition?

Journey · Preparing · Investing · Adjusting · Welcoming · Celebrating

Final prayer and blessing

We bless God for the example of Joseph:
for his humility before the greatness of God's plans;
for his love and loyalty to Mary and Jesus;
for his willingness to change and adapt his life
so that the greatness of others might flourish.
We pray for ourselves that, in our turn,
we might be attentive listeners to God's word
and accomplish God's will in our lives.
Amen.

May the Lord bless us through the course of our life
and accompany us in all our ways.
May he favour us with deep faith and hope,
that we be might be alert not only to the God of yesterday,
but to the God of today and tomorrow,
the one who is Alpha and Omega.
Amen.

Welcoming the unforeseen

Fourth week in Advent

Welcoming the unforeseen

Mary, the surprised maiden

The ark of the covenant

One of the abiding mysteries of sacred history is what happened to the lost ark of the covenant. This enigma, which still captivates the imagination of a wide variety of people, inspired the 1981 film *Raiders of the Lost Ark*, which was set in 1936. The hero, Dr Henry Walton "Indiana" Jones, is played by Harrison Ford. Indiana Jones is a distinguished archaeologist and college professor who has a more adventurous sideline as an explorer and mercenary. He is assigned by government agents to locate the ark of the covenant before the Nazis discover it and use it to further their ascendancy. The Nazis are seeking the ark in the belief that it will make them invincible like the Israelites in the Old Testament, who revered it not only for holding the Ten Commandments but as the dwelling place of God on earth. While Indiana succeeds in recovering the ark in Egypt, the Nazis manage to steal it and capture Indiana. When the Nazis perform a ceremony to open the ark, they are all killed gruesomely by the ark's ancient curse on anyone who would interfere with its integrity. Indiana, who survives this curse simply by closing his eyes, manages to get the ark back to the United States,

where it is stored, unsurprisingly, in a secret government warehouse.

Where there are gaps in history, popular belief and muscular imagination are often ready to supply explanations. The story of the ark of the covenant goes back to Moses, the great lawgiver, celebrated in the Hebrew scriptures as the only human being to have set eyes on God. After receiving the Ten Commandments from God on tablets of stone, Moses descended Mount Sinai to see that his brother, Aaron, had melted a stockpile of gold collected from the people and moulded it into the effigy of a calf, building an altar before the golden idol. The assembled Israelites then offered holocausts and brought communion sacrifices (Exodus 32:1-6). Moses, in anger and protest, broke the tablets of stone (Exodus 32:19).

God later inscribed two other tablets, to replace the ones Moses smashed. This second set, brought down from Mount Sinai by Moses, was to be placed in the ark of the covenant, which was also designated the "ark of the testimony". According to the tradition God commanded Moses to have a special ark made (Exodus 25:10-

22; 37:1-9), the instructions being specific about material, dimensions and design. The ark was a chest of two and a half cubits in length, by one and a half cubits in height, by one and a half cubits in width – a cubit being about eighteen inches.

It was constructed of setim wood (an incorruptible acacia) and was plated with pure gold, inside and out. Covering the box was the *kapporeth*, of pure gold, that also formed the base for two sculpted cherubim, also made of pure gold. The two cherubim faced one another, and their wings, which wrapped around their bodies, formed a canopy for the throne of God. It is worth noting that this is the only exception to the law forbidding the Israelites to make carved images, an exception rendered reasonably harmless to the faith of the people because the ark was regularly kept inside the tabernacle, surrounded by heavy curtains. The gold covering between the two cherubim was the throne of mercy, the meeting place with God:

"The cherubim shall spread out their wings above, overshadowing the mercy-seat with their wings... You shall put the mercy-seat on the top of the ark; and in the ark you shall put the covenant that I shall give you. There I will meet you, and from above the mercy-seat, from between the two cherubim that are on the ark of the covenant, I will deliver to you all my commands for the Israelites."
(Exodus 25:20-22)

On the body of the ark, four gold rings were attached, through which two poles, also made of acacia and coated in gold, were placed: these were never to be moved. The family of Kohath, of the tribe of Levi, were to carry the ark on their shoulders using these poles. (We can catch something of what the ark looked like from the artist's impression – although the artist forgot to show the poles covered in gold.) The contents of the ark have been debated through the centuries. The general consensus is that the tablets containing the Ten Commandments were placed inside

together with a golden vessel containing manna, the food from heaven (Exodus 16:34), and the rod of Aaron which had blossomed as a sign of his priesthood (Numbers 17:10).

This most important symbol of the Jewish faith served as the only physical manifestation of God on earth. The legends associated with the ark, and the harsh penalties prescribed for anyone who misused it, confirm its centrality to the Jewish faith of that period. When Solomon's Temple was completed, Solomon, before the dedication, assembled the elders of Israel to convey the ark from the place where David had set it up to the Holy of Holies, its true home (1 Kings 8:1-12). After Solomon's reign all the other sacred shrines in Israel were destroyed, following the belief that God had only one address on earth, and could only be properly worshipped there.

The memory of the ark's sacredness, however, was to pass away. In 587 BC, at the fall of Jerusalem, the ark disappeared for ever. One tradition says that it was hidden in a secret vault beneath the Temple mount, one constructed for that very purpose. In the Apocalypse of Esdras,

the ark of the covenant is reported to have been taken by the victorious army that ransacked Jerusalem (2 Esdras 10:20-22). This is in keeping with 2 Kings 25, which reports that the Babylonian troops carried away from the Temple whatever brass, silver and gold they could lay their hands upon, although it has to be said that the ark is not listed among the spoils taken from the Temple. It was a popular belief among the ancient rabbis that the ark would be found at the coming of the Messiah. The ark is never mentioned among the sacred objects of the Second Temple.

For the prophet Jeremiah, the ark's presence in the Temple gave the priests and people a false sense of security about God's presence among them. That presence, Jeremiah argued, was neither permanent nor guaranteed. Whatever happened to the ark, Jeremiah, in one of his prophecies referring to the messianic times, announced that it would be utterly forgotten: "It shall not come to mind, or be remembered, or missed; nor shall another one be made" (Jeremiah 3:16).

The silence surrounding the ark, in accordance with Jeremiah's prophecy, can be heard in the remainder of the Old Testament. That silence is broken by Luke in the New Testament. Uniquely among the evangelists, it is Luke who presents Mary as the ark of the new covenant. Now the power of the Most High will overshadow a consecrated person rather than a consecrated place. Mary will become the sacred vessel that hosts the presence of God. Although we are familiar with tabernacles in churches, Mary is the first tabernacle of God that is made not of gold or silver or bronze but of human flesh. The womb of this woman, not a golden box carried exclusively by priests, will be the home of the Son of God.

Welcoming

Gospel text: Luke 1:26-38

In the sixth month the angel Gabriel was sent by God to a town in Galilee called Nazareth, to a virgin engaged to a man whose name was Joseph, of the house of David. The virgin's name was Mary.

And he came to her and said, "Greetings, favoured one! The Lord is with you." But she was much perplexed by his words and pondered what sort of greeting this might be.

The angel said to her, "Do not be afraid, Mary, for you have found favour with God. And now, you will conceive in your womb and bear a son, and you will name him Jesus. He will be great, and will be called the Son of the Most High, and the Lord God will give to him the throne of his ancestor David. He will reign over the house of Jacob for ever, and of his kingdom there will be no end."

Mary said to the angel, "How can this be, since I am a virgin?" The angel said to her, "The Holy Spirit will come upon you, and the power of the Most High will overshadow you; therefore the child to be born will be holy; he will be called Son of God. And now, your relative Elizabeth in her old age has also conceived a son; and this is the sixth month for her who was said to be barren. For nothing will be impossible with God."

Then Mary said, "Here am I, the servant of the Lord; let it be with me according to your word." Then the angel departed from her.

Journey — Preparing — Investing — Adjusting — Welcoming — Celebrating

Welcoming

Reflecting on the Gospel story

Two annunciations

When the evangelist John celebrates the beginning of the Jesus story in his prologue, he rewrites the opening of Genesis to proclaim that the Word of God at the beginning was not just an effective word that created what it said: this Word was a person who existed from the beginning in God; indeed, this Word was God. In the light of the Jesus story John believes that not only the story of creation and humanity, but the very idea of God has to be rewritten to catch up with the startling new things that have been accomplished in Jesus. Who Jesus emerged to be, John will argue, forces believers to revise everything they took for granted beforehand: in Jesus our understanding of everything has to be updated.

This Word, John proclaims, was the creator of all things and the ancestor of all that lives – he belonged first to eternity, but was coming into the world that had its being through him: "And the Word became flesh" (John 1:14). The account is spare and free from any historical detail or witness: no mother is introduced, no time is recorded, no place is noted, and no witnesses are named – because, for this evangelist, Jesus'

beginning is beyond the cosmos and history in the fullness of God.

By way of dramatic contrast, when Luke celebrates the beginning of the Jesus story, he wants to celebrate the beginning of a human story, not a cosmic story. All human stories begin the same, inevitably involving the particularity of time and date ("in the days of King Herod of Judea") and place ("a town in Galilee called Nazareth"), as well as other human beings. Luke knows that Jesus does not come as a bolt from the blue, but he comes, as we all come, through the womb of a mother. To celebrate the birth of Jesus you need a particular woman: you need Mary of Nazareth. Luke brings Mary centre stage at the beginning of his Gospel: while Joseph enjoys that position at the beginning of Matthew's Gospel, Luke reserves this centrality for Mary of Nazareth.

Six months after interrupting Zechariah in the Temple, Gabriel startles a young fiancée at home in Nazareth in Galilee. Since angels normally "appear" without warning, their sudden and spectacular entrances are calculated to alarm people who are going about their daily life. Clearly angels have a

charism for fright, which is probably why, wherever they go, they are always urging their flabbergasted clients, "Do not be afraid." They announce a new beginning, one that will take their listeners on an unforeseen path and change their lives for ever.

Two paintings
As the story of John the Baptist begins in sacred space, in the Temple, in the midst of solemn ritual, the story of Jesus will transpire in ordinary space, where people are going about their normal business. This is why I've chosen John Collier's painting *The Annunciation* as the image to introduce this chapter. Collier is a modern American sculptor and painter, a convert Catholic, who now specialises in religious works. Like the old masters before him, he sets the scene at the time of painting, not the time of the event. This is not Nazareth in the ancient world but suburbia in today's world. Mary is a picture of innocence, a schoolgirl dressed in her school uniform, wearing saddle shoes, standing on the welcome mat of her home.

She is interrupted on her own doorstep while dutifully reading – possibly her homework?

She doesn't look frightened by her deferential visitor with a neat haircut, whose full robe fashionably matches his wings; she appears more bemused, suspecting perhaps that he has arrived at the wrong address. Clearly Gabriel has not yet said anything; Mary is still holding her book at the ready. This young girl is the picture of suburban serenity. If she is worried about what the neighbours will think, she doesn't show it. We wonder if Gabriel has just delivered the large pot of lily flowers, signifying purity, which are about to blossom. Collier manages to depict with unusual tenderness both the ordinariness of the setting and the extraordinariness of the event.

In contrast there is *The Annunciation* by Henry Ossawa Tanner, painted in 1898. The son of a bishop in the African Methodist Episcopal Church, Tanner painted *The Annunciation* soon after returning to Paris from a trip to Egypt and Palestine in 1898. Tanner specialised in religious subjects, and wanted to experience the people, culture, architecture and light of the Holy Land. After returning from his travels, Tanner created this scene of the annunciation from images that impressed themselves on his mind.

Mary is shown as an adolescent dressed in Middle Eastern peasant clothing, without a halo. The angel Gabriel appears as a dazzling shaft of light permeating the room with its glow. In the intimacy of her bedroom Mary is awakened from sleep, her bedcovers now thrown aside. We see fragile humanity, in a rumpled setting, before angelic brilliance – the meeting of two different worlds. We watch this young girl, her head inclined, holding her breath, her hands clasped together, her feet firmly on the floor, as she attends to the angel's command: "Listen!" We see Mary listening, listening, listening, with her whole body: she is the embodiment of stillness and unmixed attention, a portrait of true receptive prayer.

The poet and philosopher John O'Donohue could have been commenting on this painting when he wrote:

> "In the morning it takes the mind a while
> To find the world again, lost after dream
> Has taken the heart to the underworld
> To play with the shades of lives not chosen.
>
> She awakens a stranger in her own life,
> Her breath loud in the room full of listening.
> Taken without touch, her flesh feels the grief
> Of belonging to what cannot be seen."[1]

The angel's annunciation

Mary is going about her daily business when her life is interrupted by something not of her own choosing. Unlike the ancient couple, Zechariah and Elizabeth, the young Mary in Luke's Gospel is neither yearning nor praying for a child; she is waiting to move in with her husband, at which point their marriage will be completed, with the expectation that they will have marital relations in the hope of beginning a family. Luke's story of the annunciation celebrates the initiative and approach of God: the focus is on the surprise appearance of God's messenger and the message, not on the need or aspirations of Mary. This birth proposal is God's original idea. This child comes not as the answer to a couple's prayer but as the gratuitous act of God.

When, like Zechariah, Mary interrupts the angel – to point out that she has had no relations with a man – Gabriel does not punish her intervention. Gabriel is much nicer to young girls than he is to old priests, and he explains:

> "The Holy Spirit will come upon you, and the power of the Most High will overshadow you; therefore the child to be born will be holy; he will be called Son of God."
> (Luke 1:35)

Mary's objection points to her state as a virgin: she has never had sexual relations. Mary's virginity is important because it points beyond herself, to a new creation, a birth in which God's Spirit that was active in the original creation of life is now active again. In the opening of Genesis the writer describes the vast emptiness: "the earth was a formless void and darkness covered the face of the deep, while [the spirit of

[1] J. O'Donohue, *Conamara Blues* (London: Doubleday, 2000), 46.

God] swept over the face of the waters" (Genesis 1:2). Just as the earth was a void in the beginning, so Mary's womb is a void: that void will be filled by the creative act of God's Spirit in the gift of God's Son. That act will earn Mary the first title she was accorded by the Church: *theotokos*, God-bearer, the one who tabernacles the Son of God.

Mary's annunciation

The angel's explanation is followed by a sign: that Mary's kinswoman, even in her old age, has conceived a son – Elizabeth, who was known to be barren, is now in her sixth month. Mary does not check out the truth of the sign before she gives her response; she gives the ready response of the disciple when challenged by the word of God: "let it be with me according to your word" (Luke 1:38).

That is *her* annunciation, her consent to hand over her body and spirit to God's purpose. For the story of Jesus to be told, it needs more than God's word to be spoken; it also needs the human word to say yes. In the annunciation Luke shows us that the God who chooses Mary must wait on Mary's own response. The love that offers itself is the love that must wait. Even God

has to wait; even God has to hold his breath; even God needs permission from a mother-to-be if God's saving plan is to go ahead. That is why there are two annunciations: God's annunciation to Mary, then Mary's annunciation to God. God's best plans can only happen when there is human cooperation, when God's word and our word come together. When those two annunciations come together, God's word always takes flesh.

Whatever Mary was planning for her life with Joseph, it did not include becoming pregnant outside that relationship. If she ever dreamed of being a princess, she knew that as a peasant girl she was destined to marry a carpenter. Then an unexpected word interrupts the routine of ordinary time and proposes a groundbreaking diversion from what is planned; nothing less than a startling new future is proposed. Will Mary stay with her own domestic plans or risk an uncharted adventure as God's collaborator? Mary's annunciation to the angel enshrines her response in consenting to the word of God happening in her: "Here am I, the servant of the Lord" (Luke 1:38). Mary gives up her own wishes and adopts God's desire; she gives up personal control of her life in favour of God's promise; in her

response she pledges her body and spirit to the purposes of God. Mary welcomes the unforeseen and adjusts her life to this new adventure.

Mary's response is unparalleled in the other annunciation narratives: she is the one who when hearing the word of God gladly allows that word to form her life. Later, her son will say during his public ministry: "My mother and my brothers are those who hear the word of God and do it" (Luke 8:21). Mary is now presented as the perfect disciple who is a hearer of the word and a doer of the word. With that response, the angel takes his leave. Thus Mary becomes the literal embodiment of the promise of God: she conceives the promise, she becomes pregnant with the promise, and she will give birth to the promise. And the promise will be called "holy... the Son of God".

Welcoming the unforeseen

How do you walk on an unmapped road, in the fog, with confidence? There are no antique maps, previously charted, to guide you on the way. There are no people to consult who have experienced the challenge you are now facing, no experts to guide you with their shared wisdom.

No one has walked this road before you. Nobody. You have no idea where the road will end, what you will confront on the way; you can only imagine how you will manage. You might wonder: did you say yes too quickly, agree too readily to take this unforeseen road? Should you have asked more questions? Should you have insisted on more guidance? Do you look behind you as you notice that what was once familiar territory is now rapidly disappearing in the fog? Will there be a way back to the uncomplicated life you left behind you? And another question hovers over everything for Mary: not what will this child turn out to be, but how will she and Joseph manage his upbringing? How do you mother the Son of God?

Sometimes the only way we can learn is by doing, setting out, leaving the cautious voices behind us, even though we might still be afraid of our own inexperience and inadequacy. There is no rehearsal, we know, only live performance. We have to trust that voice within, the voice that we have discovered is truly ours, and head out to welcome the unforeseen. And we might know that we are not wholly alone in this new adventure.

At the beginning of his Gospel Luke celebrates that something radically new is going to happen: because of God's initiative and a young girl's "Yes" to the unforeseen, the presence of God is going to become vulnerable in human flesh. In the ancient days it was the ark of the covenant that marked the presence of God; the nearness of God was symbolised by the empty space between the cherubim on the ark. Emptiness. Now, Luke says, something new is going to happen. The presence of God is going to take human shape in the womb of Mary. Mary of Nazareth is the tabernacle of God.

Mary, like all mothers, gives over her body and mind and soul so that new life may be born. She does that so that a life larger than hers may take its own place in the world. All mothers must wait for the gradual process that is happening within them; they must learn to let go of the child within them. They must not only nurture the presence of the child within them; they must nurture the leaving of the child. The act of childbirth is the painful act of letting go, so that the life within can take its own separate place in the world. Mary's vocation is not only to hold Jesus within her but also to let him go, let him become the person he must become.

Mary assists the struggle of God to be one like us. There is something dangerously new about Mary. She is the woman at the centre of the Christian story, essential to this new beginning. It is a woman, not a man, who brings God's real presence into the world. Through her the presence of the *Christos Kyrios* will be known and celebrated.

Another annunciation

As the pain of mothers does not stop in the act of giving birth, neither does Mary's. As the Gospel opened in Jerusalem, so the action returns there in Luke's account of the presentation of Jesus in the Temple, where the new family is welcomed by two ancient figures, the prophet Simeon and the prophetess Anna (Luke 2:22-38).

The new family honouring the Law provides the occasion and the setting for moving the action to the Jerusalem Temple. In the Mosaic Law a woman was regarded as ritually unclean for forty days after the birth of a male child. At the end of that time she was required to present herself to a priest for the rite of purification; she was to make her offering to the priest at the door of the sanctuary (Leviticus 12:6-8). Although Luke speaks of "their" purification, the

Journey — Preparing · Investing · Adjusting · Welcoming · Celebrating

Law required only the mother's (Leviticus 12:2). Mary is shown to be obedient to the Law, and in its fulfilment makes the offering of the poor: two turtle-doves or two pigeons.

As Israel was ready to die when he had looked on the face of his lost son, Joseph (Genesis 46:30), so Simeon is now prepared to die because he has seen the fulfilment of the Lord's promise in Jesus. In spite of being an old man, Simeon looks forward, not backwards, to the consolation of Israel. He is not captivated by the past, but attentive to the present moment. With this visit there is no reason for Simeon to wait any longer, any more than there is for a watchman to stay at his post after the arrival of the one expected: the visit that was promised by God and expected by the faithful of Israel has taken place in history.

Simeon's mission is completed when he can see in this child the anointed of God: in a sense the old Israel can now depart in peace because a new era is beginning. Simeon's own fulfilment is bound to the fulfilment of God's plan, and that mutual fulfilment is something that Jesus expresses to his disciples: "Blessed are the eyes that see what you see! For I tell you that many

prophets and kings desired to see what you see, but did not see it" (Luke 10:23-24). Simeon sees "it" in the person of Jesus.

Luke recounts that Mary and Joseph are astonished at what Simeon says. This might appear surprising since Mary has already been told of the stature of the child in the annunciation, and both she and Joseph have been told of the angel's annunciation to the shepherds. Why then the surprise? This has led some scholars to argue that the annunciation, the nativity and the presentation are separate traditions, none of which supposes the existence of the others. But it is possible to see the surprise of Mary and Joseph as a Lucan device to underline something of supreme importance: a prophet guided by the Spirit has just revealed to Mary and Joseph something that has not been contained in the previous revelations – the significance of Jesus for the Gentile world.

Adding a more specific note to the oracle, Simeon addresses Mary and foretells how the child will be a source of division in Israel, something that Jesus will voice in his own preaching when he refers to the division he is sent to cause in families (Luke 12:51-53). He will be the occasion for the

fall of many people and the rise of many, and a sign destined to be rejected by Israel (Acts 2:22-23). Not only does Mary hear that her son is destined to be rejected but that a sword will pierce her own soul (Luke 2:35). That is a very painful annunciation to hear about your son's future and your own.

Facing the pain

Mary will be seriously wounded because of her child, a truth captured exquisitely in

Mantegna's painting of *The Presentation of Christ in the Temple*. As we look at the painting, we feel we have stumbled on a very private moment, spotted through an open window. We absorb the details. We notice that Simeon is not looking at the extraordinary child wrapped in swaddling clothes but at his mother; his eyes seem to drill through her like the words he has just spoken. Joseph, with furrowed brow, looks sternly at Simeon: they have not come to the Temple to hear such tormented prophecy. The two witnesses look away in hopeless politeness as if what they've just heard is too private and, therefore, best left unattended. Her right elbow anchored on the window as she holds her child, Mary lowers her eyes, pensively, looking at Simeon's closed lips – did he just say that? She has just heard something as personal as it is painful. We are left to wonder as we walk away.

This painting is an extraordinary insight into the conflict that is part of Mary's motherhood. While Gabriel told Zechariah that his son would be a joy and delight – every father's dream – Mary hears a different annunciation from Simeon, that her son will be like a sword driven through her soul – every mother's nightmare. Mary hears two annunciations about her son: one from an angel that listed his future accomplishments; and now one from an old prophet telling her that her son will be cast aside and she will be deeply wounded because of him. How do you hold these two annunciations together?

There is a sense, especially among us Catholics, that when we think of Mary we sometimes think of her as an uncritical supporter of everything her son does in life, cheering him on to the final act of shameful crucifixion, as if she didn't have a mind of her own or was incapable of seeing things differently from him. Yet Simeon's prophecy warns of the future hurt she will surely know in her body and spirit. Mary is not a plastic cheerleader on the sidelines of Jesus' life; she is his mother witnessing a painful gradual revelation.

Mary will see how at the beginning of Jesus' public ministry, especially after the execution of John the Baptist, it looks *possible* that her son will pay a similar fatal price for the choices he is making and the powerful people he is criticising. Then she will notice, soon enough, that his death looks *likely* as he develops his considerable charism for making enemies. And finally, too soon, as she watches her hill-country son head south for the city of Jerusalem, she will admit to herself that his execution is *inevitable* because he is unwavering in his course of action.

Sometimes I imagine a scene in Nazareth during Jesus' ministry: a neighbour of Mary returns from pilgrimage in Jerusalem to tell her that he shared a table with her son in the house of a leading Pharisee. Mary leans forward, hungry for the detail of fresh news. The neighbour recounts how Jesus not only compared the Pharisees to unmarked tombs that contaminated everyone who came near them but also went on to criticise the lawyers for imposing unendurable burdens on ordinary people. Jesus, he reports, dismissed all the religious people at table not only as hypocritical but as fatal to people's health. Mary's neighbour concludes his account by noting that when Jesus left the house, the scribes and the Pharisees began a furious attack on him (see Luke 11:37-54).

How do you think Mary would react to this news? Do you imagine her cheering on her son stubbornly or wishing that her beloved son would retire from his campaign and take up fishing? Most mothers want, above all things, security and safety for their children. No mother wants to see her son, whatever age he is, move into harm's way while effortlessly making powerful enemies who will have the last word, one that will be spoken with final and fatal authority.

Certainly in the course of her life Mary will have abundant reasons to pause and ponder things in her heart. But the prophecy of Simeon lies in the future, referring to what this child will become. This is a warning that the choices her son will make, the friends he will gather around him, his abiding love for the last and the least and the lost, the upside-down values he will profess, and the enemies he will attract, will all cause her pain. While this prophecy does not necessarily argue to Mary's disapproval of what her son will do, it recognises how the painful consequences of his choices will affect her.

And yet Mary's "Yes" in her annunciation was, by definition, a yes to the unseen and the unimaginable. When she declared her fiat she could not have known everything that her yes entailed, any more than anyone who stands at the altar and solemnly promises "till death us do part" knows what the unseen journey of marriage will involve. Promises are made in the fog.

Journey — Preparing — Investing — Adjusting — Welcoming — Celebrating

The words we say, certainly at the time of saying, are important as we aim ourselves into an unknown future. In a poem called "Their Lonely Betters", the poet W.H. Auden sits in a chair in his garden, listens to the rustling flowers, looks at the robins, and thinks about what the difference is between what he sees and hears and what we as humans do:

> "Not one of them was capable of lying,
> There was not one which knew that it
>   was dying
> Or could have with a rhythm or a rhyme
> Assumed responsibility for time.
> Let them leave language to their lonely
>   betters
> Who count some days and long for
>   certain letters;
> We, too, make noises when we laugh or
>   weep:
> Words are for those with promises to
>   keep."[2]

"Words are for those with promises to keep" highlights the weight of words and the human accountability that follows from using them. Sometimes the words we use are much bigger than our capacity to deliver; at other times we manage to struggle into fidelity and enflesh the promises we make.

We celebrate Mary not only as a maker of promises but as a keeper of promises. She fosters this child within her and then shares him with a waiting world. This child is her own, but not entirely her own: he is given, as Simeon prophesied, as a light to enlighten all peoples. That is why we celebrate Mary as a model for all Christians. As Christians we are challenged to carry Christ, not in wombs, but in hearts and minds, into the dark places of the world; to carry him to those who are broken and hurt and wounded, those who are dying to hear good news. While we celebrate Mary as the unique *theotokos*, we are pledged to be God-bearers ourselves and to share the Christ within us as liberating Gospel.

[2] W.H. Auden, *Collected Poems*, ed. Edward Mendelson (New York: Random House, 1976), 444.

Welcoming

Questions for reflection

1. There is an old criticism of Catholics that we "worship" Mary and give her much more attention than she receives in the Gospels or in the early writing of the Church. How would you answer this objection?

2. Have another look at the two paintings of the annunciation by John Collier and Henry Ossawa Tanner. Give yourself time to absorb the details. Which of the paintings do you prefer? Is there anything you see in them that shocks you, puzzles you, or delights you?

3. If you were commissioned to design a new tabernacle for use in a church, one that was based on Luke's portrait of Mary as the ark of the new covenant, what would your tabernacle look like?

4. Sometimes we plan our future through the choices we make; at other times things happen to us and we find ourselves with no other option than to take new roads. Are you the kind of person that is open to the future or are you suspicious of anything that you haven't planned yourself?

5. Has there ever been a time in your life when you felt that God was calling you to take a new direction in your life, one that you never anticipated? If so, when did it happen? And what did you decide to do?

Final prayer and blessing

Remember, O most gracious Virgin Mary,
that never was it known
that anyone who fled to your protection,
implored your help,
or sought your intercession was left unaided.
Inspired by this confidence, we fly to you,
O virgin of virgins, our Mother.
To you we come;
before you we stand, sinful and sorrowful.
O Mother of the Word incarnate,
despise not our petitions,
but in your mercy hear and answer us.
Amen.

(The Memorare)

I arise today
Through a mighty strength:
God's power to guide me,
God's might to uphold me,
God's eyes to watch over me;
God's ear to hear me,
God's word to give me speech,
God's hand to guard me,
God's way to lie before me,
God's shield to shelter me,
God's host to secure me.

(St Patrick's Breastplate)

Celebrating new beginnings
Christmas

Celebrating new beginnings

Belonging

A sense of the particular

Everyone was born of particular parents, in a particular place on the map, and at a particular time in history. Think for a moment of your own childhood – of the people who supported you and surrounded you, the place where you grew up, and the kind of time you had – and how all these have influenced who you have become. We all have about us a sense of the particular which gives some form to our identity and some shape to our sense of who we are. Our own roots give us a sense of belonging – affiliated to a mixed bag of people and belonging to places that may make no impression on others but are special to us because they mark the address of our childhood.

Sometimes we return to hunt for the leftovers of childhood; we try to uncover our roots to understand the kind of people we have become. This probably doesn't happen to us before our mid thirties. When I was working on my book *The Parables of Jesus*,[1] reflecting on why Jesus used fictional stories at the heart of his teaching, I found myself going back to my childhood to rediscover a love of story. In the introduction to the book I wrote about my mother and her strange ability to connect with a litany of quirky people through her interest in story.

Her natural sense of drama, her delight in the awkward and the eccentric, the crooked and the cracked, seemed to disqualify her as a reporter of the sheer ordinariness of life. Yet her observations, as we found out as children, were often stunningly accurate. So I wanted to credit that, to acknowledge it, to say that who I am is determined to a large extent by my upbringing and my roots. I came from her; I caught her lust for language and observation; I owe her, among many other things, for those shared interests.

It's funny how, when people want to know who we are, the question often comes: "Where are you from?" Perhaps it's because the land we come from offers the first clue to others of our hidden identity. When we name the place, some people will delight in it; others will look mystified; others will be frankly disappointed. In the eyes of some people geography disables you: "Can anything good come out of Nazareth?" (John 1:46). Whatever the reaction about where we come from, it's as if people need to register us in place and in time before they can really grow to know us. Perhaps the same is true of God: perhaps God must register in place and in time before we can grow to know God and love God.

[1] D. McBride, *The Parables of Jesus* (Chawton: Redemptorist Publications, 1999).

Celebrating

Gospel text: Luke 2:1-20

In those days a decree went out from Emperor Augustus that all the world should be registered. This was the first registration and was taken while Quirinius was governor of Syria. All went to their own towns to be registered. Joseph also went from the town of Nazareth in Galilee to Judea, to the city of David called Bethlehem, because he was descended from the house and family of David. He went to be registered with Mary, to whom he was engaged and who was expecting a child. While they were there, the time came for her to deliver her child. And she gave birth to her firstborn son and wrapped him in bands of cloth, and laid him in a manger, because there was no place for them in the inn.

In that region there were shepherds living in the fields, keeping watch over their flock by night. Then an angel of the Lord stood before them, and the glory of the Lord shone around them, and they were terrified. But the angel said to them, "Do not be afraid; for see – I am bringing you good news of great joy for all the people: to you is born this day in the city of David a Saviour, who is the Messiah, the Lord. This will be a sign for you: you will find a child wrapped in bands of cloth and lying in a manger." And suddenly there was with the angel a multitude of the heavenly host, praising God and saying,

"Glory to God in the highest heaven,
and on earth peace among those whom he
favours!"

When the angels had left them and gone into heaven, the shepherds said to one another, "Let us go now to Bethlehem and see this thing that has taken place, which the Lord has made known to us." So they went with haste and found Mary and Joseph, and the child lying in the manger. When they saw this, they made known what had been told them about this child; and all who heard it were amazed at what the shepherds told them. But Mary treasured all these words and pondered them in her heart. The shepherds returned, glorifying and praising God for all they had heard and seen, as it had been told them.

Journey — Preparing — Investing — Adjusting — Welcoming — Celebrating

Celebrating

Reflecting on the Gospel story

The visitors get centre stage

One of the peculiar things about the two Gospel stories of Jesus' birth is that the account of the birth doesn't take up much space in the narrative. The birth is narrated in half a line by Matthew: "she had borne a son; and he named him Jesus" (Matthew 1:25). Luke is fulsome by comparison, having two sentences: "While they were there, the time came for her to deliver her child. And she gave birth to her firstborn son and wrapped him in bands of cloth, and laid him in a manger, because there was no place for them in the inn" (Luke 2:6-7). Like the death of Jesus, the birth of Jesus is passed over in language that is surprisingly spare for such a momentous event. There is no detail of this dramatic birth, no reaction noted from Mary or Joseph, no voices – not even a cry – from the three main characters. Like the death of Jesus, the story of his birth is told through the eyes of the observers, those who come from near or far to witness the event.

The two Gospel narratives shift the spotlight away from the birth to focus attention on those who look on the event – not the immediate family, interestingly, but outsiders. We are invited to see the events through the eyes of two different groups: the shepherds in Luke's Gospel and the wise men in Matthew's. For the evangelists it is these witnesses who appear large; it is they who take centre stage and respond to what they see and hear.

The shepherds are Bethlehem locals, poor people, who are watching their flocks by night. You might think that these stargazers would be the ones to clock a new star as it lit up the night sky; instead they are graced with an angelic annunciation, surrounded by the glory of God, and treated to a bravura performance of five-part angelic choirs singing the Gloria! The wise men, by contrast, are foreign celebrities, people of substance, who gain ready access to the palace of King Herod and can converse with majesty and his counsellors. The magi come from the mysterious east, which long before Christianity had been the birthplace of many religions. These wise men follow a new star in the sky; for all their exotic importance, there are no angelic choirs for them. They are excited about what is new and fresh and unexplained. Eventually they reach their destination in a child, offer their unconventional gifts, and kneel down to worship.

Journey   Preparing   Investing   Adjusting   Welcoming   Celebrating

If the wise men represent the wisdom of the world, the shepherds represent the poor people of the world, the nobodies, those who are marginalised. Shepherds belonged to a despised profession – bracketed with tax collectors and moneylenders. In ancient days, when the Israelite people were nomadic, the shepherd was used as an image of a wandering God who led God's people to new pastures. That image reflected their life situation at the time and how they saw themselves. But when the people came to be landed and settled, they embraced different values: security, not freedom, became their governing value. They built a house for God, so that, like them, God could have a fixed address. The wandering shepherd was now a reminder of their troubled past; he was also a threat to their private property.

Regarded popularly as thieves, shepherds led their herds onto other people's lands, pilfering the product of the land, wilfully blind to signs saying "No Trespassing" because they believed that God was the real landowner. They were tough men – nothing meek and mild about them – who had to fight against jackals and robbers and each other. There was no law of the sabbath for them. There was no law other than the law of the wilderness, what we would call the law of the jungle. Given the months they would live in the hill country and out in the wilderness, they would be unwashed and dirty – not a ritual pool in sight. They would be familiar with loneliness in a landscape empty of people. Protective of their sheep, they were ever ready for a brawl with anyone who looked threatening. You would not invite them to afternoon tea.

It is as representatives of the marginalised people, whose voice is of no account, that the despised shepherds make their way to the manger. They bring nothing with them. Often cribs show them bringing a gentle lamb or wild flowers or fruit, but this is not in the Gospel text. Unlike the wise men, it is not their gifts or their wisdom that they bring: they bring their poverty of spirit, their poverty of reputation, their poverty of character. They represent the kind of people that Jesus will have a special heart for in his later ministry, his "ain folk".

The wise men know how to consult the heavens and how to worship with expensive gifts. The shepherds come empty-handed because they have nothing to offer but themselves. They rejoice in finding one so close to their own poverty, one whose first resting place on earth is an emergency landing – what is available at the time – a borrowed feeding trough for animals. The shepherds can see that this child, for all the angelic choirs and polyphony that accompany his birth, looks like one of them. They have been told something amazing: that this child is born "to you" (Luke 2:11). He is theirs. After all, this is the town of David; this is the place celebrated in memory of the young boy David who was first overlooked because he was the little one out minding the sheep. Just as they were before all this happened.

If the clever magi are to be admired, the poor shepherds are not to be despised. They are the first group to whom the Gospel is announced; they are the first to respond graciously. The magi who had access to the palace of a king have eventually to flee from a despot: they become unwilling fugitives. Their way led them through the palace of a king to the newborn child, but they cannot return by the same route. The shepherds can go back to their fields; they are a threat to nobody. No one will be seeking their counsel.

Two different groups. Which group do we feel more comfortable with? Are we more at ease with the clever wise men, in their embroidered silken robes, who can read the stars and can afford to travel through countries to follow their dream? Or are we happier in the company of the shepherds, first terrified and then delighted, who leave their posts and follow the angel's instructions, to pay their respects to this newborn child? Whichever group we feel more at home with, we today are the witnesses, the watchers, who will always outnumber the principal characters in the drama. This Christmas we turn up, but we do more than watch. Empty-handed or not, we come to worship this little one.

God's particulars in Jesus
In this little one Luke gives us the icon of the living God, who enters history in the closing years of the reign of King Herod. In his story Luke registers the birth of Jesus as a child of a particular family, at a particular

time in history, and on a particular place on the map. The Gospel of John announces: "the Word became flesh and lived among us" (John 1:14) – without detail of family or place or time. Instead of proclamation, Luke tells a story: he introduces us to Mary and Joseph. Rather than declaring theology, Luke's narrative shows us that Jesus does not arrive in history as a traveller without baggage, who must choose a name, a family, a past, a whole identity for himself. Before he arrives, he already belongs.

Before any child arrives in life, he or she has to belong: if the belonging isn't waiting, the arrival is for ever fractured. The child will spend the rest of his or her life hunting for what was missing, and will never find it because the first belonging was never there. With all the nurture and care the child has received in the womb, every child is primed for an assured welcome, confident that he or she is heading out of a warm hiding place to an expectant world of hospitality and embrace, what we normally call family and home.

Jesus is not rootless, but is born a member of a specific tribe; he does not begin from zero, but enters an unfolding history between a yesterday and a tomorrow; he does not invent himself, but will discover himself as a unique link in a long line of faith. He is a Palestinian Jew born in the reign of Caesar Augustus and King Herod. He is in time and, therefore, in between times. For Luke the birth of Jesus is located in space and time, the natural boundaries of every human life story. To be human is always to be somewhere, never nowhere; it is always to exist sometime, never no time. "Once upon a time" is fairytale time; "the reign of Augustus" is real time. Luke registers the birth of Jesus as a sign of the historical reality of the visit of God, and a witness to the fulfilment of God's plan. In the person of Jesus God has visited the people. God has registered himself in place and in time. And that is why we celebrate at Christmas.

At Christmas we celebrate the love of God for us, which shows itself in the fragile bundle of the child Jesus. We celebrate our love of God through the person of Jesus. Perhaps it is true to say that we can love only what we can get our arms around. To love we need a particular name, a particular face, a particular person. And we have God's particulars in Jesus. When we look at Jesus we no longer have to guess at God: the best

of what we know about God is revealed in Jesus. This little one is the one who shows us God. And, like Mary and Joseph, we can all get our arms around the child from Bethlehem.

Maybe an important part of Christmas, as we celebrate the birth story of Jesus, is to recognise our own births – that our life is a gift that comes from God and other people; that who we are is what we owe. None of us crafted our beginnings, though we shape our later lives. None of us engineered our own early upbringing, though we generate new beginnings as we grow up. Who we are is a gift from others. If we are lucky, we know this, and we learn to share the gift of who we are with others. We don't apologise for it; we travel on it.

The child will grow up

The Christmas story celebrates the newness of a child we honour as the Son of God. This is hosanna not in the highest but in the lowest – omnipotence in low profile. The focus is not on status and power but on littleness and vulnerability. While important adults appear in the telling of the story, attention centres on the little one. He is the one hunted by a nervous King Herod; he is the one sought out by wise men from afar and shepherds from close by; he is the one adored by loving parents. He is the one we all look to with hope.

Think of Mary and Joseph looking at their new child. Like all parents, the love that they feel for their child will, inevitably, be accompanied by a measure of worry. How will our child grow up? How will he manage the unseen challenges that life will surely bring him? Will he find special people to love and cherish? Will he be able to delight in the knowledge that others love him and cherish him? Will he get a decent job? Will he settle down? Will he get married and give us a brood of grandchildren? Will he stay out of trouble? All things considered, will he have a good life and know peace?

When children arrive, they redefine you as a family; you take them into your heart; they become your main treasures. Beside the needs of your children, so much else looks irrelevant. Their fragility becomes your worry. They get hurt; you feel hurt. They succeed and shine; you rise up in splendour. They sink in disappointment, and you go down and down. They become a compass for your heart: wherever they point, you

are there. And your being there sometimes embarrasses them, and all they can say is, "Oh, Mum, please!"

The parents of Jesus remind us that it is not enough to bring Jesus into our hearts. The baby grows up, and he will take a lot of people into his expansive heart, expecting us to do likewise. And many of these people, as we learn from reading the Gospels, will be as odd as the night is long. One of the marks of Jesus' ministry is that with him everyone has a chance: he is not fixated by people's past, however sinful, but believes in people's ability to change in a grace-filled way. He takes on people's secret madness, their compulsions, their vulnerability, their disabilities, their lust, their thin resolve, and their in-laws. He takes them all in and treasures them. After a while it seems like Jesus' heart looks more like an emergency ward than a treasure room.

The trouble with the adult Jesus is that he never comes alone. He comes with a busload of strange friends, hangers-on, causes and projects. He tells us he comes as a package deal: accepting him means accepting the strange crowd with him – those who are vulnerable, broken, cracked, weak – the outsiders who live in a society that defines

people by religious propriety. These are his kind of people, who live beyond the boundaries of religious approval, and he is protective of them as if they are his trophies. We look over his shoulder, hoping for a more acceptable crowd. And he says, "No, they're already here."

I often wonder if, after Jesus grew up, Mary and Joseph became embarrassed or edgy when they came face to face with his friends and learned of his choices. Mark tells us frankly that Jesus' relatives thought he was out of his mind. A mother of five told me recently: "I despair when the kids bring their friends to the house – it's like entertaining a panorama of rejects on the move. Why can't they pick nice friends who can speak in sentences rather than just grunting?" All parents get a little anxious when their children bring their friends home for the first time. Will they be wild, polite, trustworthy? The inspection follows. We might wonder if Mary ever said to Jesus when he brought a few people back to the house: "Oh, son, where did you get them from?"

Yet in the end Mary stays with his vision and his choices. In the Gospel of John she turns up at the cross, when the world seems to crumble into this small forlorn space on the

hill of execution. Think of her cradling her dead son in her arms. It is another manger scene, but this time the child is the man, and it is the end of his earthly life, not the beginning. There are no stars to light up the afternoon darkness, no exotic foreigners with gifts, no shepherds eagerly attending. Simeon's prophecy has come in to land.

And yet the image of Mary turning up in the darkest place, to hold the body of her son, is one that has caught the loving attention of many Christians. She is a great disciple of her son, not least because her son has now become the little one. And the good news is that when we look around the world there are so many people, like Jesus and Mary, who cradle the little people in their arms:

- There are those who watch and wash the decay of old age, and although they might periodically complain, they are there.
- There are those who work with people who live in poverty, who breathe in the smells of poverty around the world and live in its shadow with kindness.
- There are those who nurse, who fetch, who listen to tortured stories, and gather those who are broken into the warmth of their understanding.

- There are those who bring humour and kindness into prisons and mental wards and broken lives.
- There are those who shrug off the meanness they receive from relatives and those around them, and struggle on, trying to do the generous thing and give others the benefit of the doubt.

There are many people who live out Jesus' adult vision, even without knowing it; many people who wouldn't even consider themselves religious but who have hearts educated by kindness. These are numbered among Jesus' kind of people. And we feel lucky when we have family and friends who struggle to borrow Jesus' eyes and share his vision, people whose kindness is stronger than their anger, people who will be there for others when things go wrong, people who encourage us to soldier on in difficult times.

Finally, one of the great portraits of Jesus in the New Testament, written before any of the Gospels, must be from Paul's letter to the Philippians:

"Christ Jesus...
though he was in the form of God,
did not regard equality with God
as something to be exploited,
but emptied himself,
taking the form of a slave,
being born in human likeness.
And being found in human form,
he humbled himself
and became obedient to the point of death –
even death on a cross."
(Philippians 2:5-8)

In the Christmas story we see Jesus emptying himself of his equality with God and becoming as we all are. When we celebrate Jesus' birth, we celebrate the beginning of that human story, his becoming as all people are. In Jesus we celebrate the best of our humanity, the beauty and strength of what we can be. In that sense Christmas belongs to all of us: it is the feast of our true humanity. G.K. Chesterton made the point well at the end of his poem "The House of Christmas":

"To an open house in the evening
Home shall men come,
To an older place than Eden
And a taller town than Rome.
To the end of the way of the wandering
star,
To things that cannot be and that are,
To the place where God was homeless
And all men are at home."[2]

Final prayer and blessing

When the song of the angels has been stilled,
when the star has gone from the night sky,
when the kings have reached their far shores,
when the shepherds have returned to their flocks,
then the work of Christmas really begins:
to find those who are lost,
to heal those who are broken in spirit,
to feed those who are hungry,
to release those who are oppressed,
to rebuild the nations torn by strife,
to bring peace among all peoples,
to bring the light of the Gospel
into the darkest corners of our world.

We pray that we might radiate the light of Christ,
through the kindliness of our presence
and the determination of our purpose,
every day of our lives.
Amen.

May the joy of the angels,
the eagerness of the shepherds,
the perseverance of the wise men,
the love of Joseph and Mary,
and the peace of the Christ child
be ours this Christmas.
And may the blessing of God almighty,
the Father, the Son, and the Holy Spirit,
rest upon us and remain with us always.
Amen.

[2] G.K. Chesterton, *Collected Poems* (New York: Dodd & Mead, 1932), 129.

Acknowledgements

The author and publishers are grateful for permission to reproduce extracts and pictures for the following material in this volume:

Preface
iStockphoto, pages 7, 8

Chapter 1
iStockphoto: pages 14, 23, 26, 29, 30

Courtesy of Wikimedia Commons and the Yorck Project: page 10, Notre Dame Cathedral at night, photographer Benh Lieu Song; page 17, Viktor Vasnetsov, *Judgement Day*, detail, fresco (St Vladimir's Cathedral, Kiev, Ukraine); page 20, Pietro Cavallini, *The Last Judgement*, detail, Saint Cecilia, Trastevere, Rome; page 25, Michelangelo, *The Last Judgement*, Sistine Chapel, Rome

Sir Edward Burne-Jones, *The Last Judgement Window*, 1897, detail, photographed by Alastair Carew-Cox: page 19

Chapter 2
Courtesy of Wikimedia Commons and the Yorck Project: page 32, Meister von Gracanica, *John the Baptist*, fresco, thirteenth century, Gracanica Monastery, Serbia; page 44, anonymous, the bust of Janus, Vatican Museum; page 47, Leonardo da Vinci, *St John the Baptist*, Louvre Museum, Paris

iStockphoto: pages 35, 38, 39, 51, 52

Edinburgh, National Gallery of Scotland (Bridgewater Loan, 1945), Nicolas Poussin, *The Sacrament of Baptism*: page 42

Chapter 3
iStockphoto: pages 57, 58

Shutterstock: page 61

Courtesy of Wikimedia Commons and the Yorck Project: page 54, Giotto di Bondone, detail, *The Nativity*; page 64, Gentile da Fabriano, *Dream of Joseph*; page 67, artist unknown, *The Three Magi before Herod*, France, early fifteenth century, stained glass; page 70, detail of the three kings from *The Adoration of the Magi*, tapestry, designed by Edward Burne-Jones with details by William Morris and John Henry Dearle; page 72, Guido da Siena, *Flight into Egypt*; page 74, Fra Angelico, Joseph, detail from the *Flight into Egypt*, panel; page 78, unknown artist, *Joseph and the child Jesus*, seventeenth century, Brooklyn Museum

Chapter 4
John Collier, *The Annunciation*, with permission from Hillstream LLC – artist's work can be seen at www.hillstream.com: page 80

Shutterstock: pages 83, 99

iStockphoto: page 93

Courtesy of Wikimedia Commons and the Yorck Project: Brooklyn Museum; page 87, Antonello da Messina, *Polyptychon of the Annunciation*, 1473, Museo Nazionale, Rome; page 90, Henry Ossawa Tanner, *The Annunciation*, painted in 1898; page 96, Andrea Mantegna, *The Presentation of Christ in the Temple*, fifteenth century; page 100, *Our Lady of the Conception*, wooden sculpture, eighteenth century, Museo Júlio de Castilhos, Porto Alegre, Brazil – photograph courtesy of Ricardo André Frantz

Chapter 5
The Holy Family, © Janet McKenzie, The Loyola School, New York, NY. For artist's work see www.JanetMcKenzie.com: page 102

Courtesy of Wikimedia Commons and the Yorck Project: page 107, stained glass, Asunción de María Church in Tenango del Valle, Mexico State, photographer Thelmadatter; pages 111 and 117, detail of the three kings from *The Adoration of the Magi*, tapestry, designed by Edward Burne-Jones with details by William Morris and John Henry Dearle; page 114, Carmen Jiménez, bust of Jesus of Nazareth in polychrome wood, Seville, Spain, 1999 – photograph by Manuel Ruiz-Garrido

iStockphoto: pages 105, 109

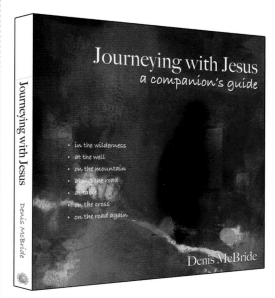
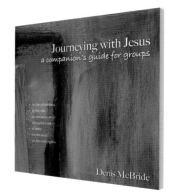